SELLING EDGE
EDGE

THE SELLING EDGE

PATRICK FORSYTH

PIATKUS

With thanks to all the clients who have said 'Yes' to me over the years – in the hope that some will do so again.

First published in 1992 by
Judy Piatkus (Publishers) Ltd
5 Windmill Street, London W1P 1HF

First paperback edition 1993

The moral right of the author has been asserted

A catalogue record for this book is
available from the British Library

ISBN 0-7499-1142-5
    0-7499-1235-9 (pbk)

Designed by Paul Saunders
Edited by Carol Franklin

Set in 10½/13pt Linotron Times by Computerset, Heathrow
Printed and bound in Great Britain by
Biddles Ltd, Guildford and King's Lynn

Contents

Acknowledgements

Buyers Are a Tough Lot

It is any buyer's job to get the best possible deal for his company. That is what they are paid for, they are not actually on the salesmen's side, and will attempt to get the better of them in every way, especially on discounts.

This is well illustrated by the apocryphal story of the fairground strongman. During his act he took an orange, put it in the crook of his arm and bending his arm squeezed the juice out. He then challenged the audience offering £10 to anyone able to squeeze out another drop.

After many had tried unsuccessfully, one apparently unlikely candidate came forward, he squeezed and squeezed and finally out came a couple more drops. The strongman was amazed, and, seeking to explain how this was possible, asked as he paid out the £10 what the man did for a living. 'I am a buyer with Ford Motor Company' he replied.

Buyers are not really like this; they are worse.

From *Everything You Need to Know about Marketing*
by Patrick Forsyth (Kogan Page, 1990)

When my first book, *Running an Effective Sales Office*, was published, I wrote at the beginning: 'Plagiarism is stealing from one person, research is stealing from many. This book is pure research (and this quotation was stolen).'

The thought remains valid, not only for this new book, but perhaps also for others in the business field. What often occurs is that ideas, approaches and principles are drawn from many sources. Many people contribute; directly and sometimes unwittingly. Always, as a consultant and trainer, one of my most important sources is client work. I have learnt a great deal from people who have commissioned courses, attended courses and contributed to their success by their participation. The whole enables an attempt to be made to set down the experience and present it in a form that may help others: in this case to sell more, with a greater success rate.

To thank all the influences of twenty years would be impossible, but, equally, to pretend they were unimportant would be wrong. They are a prerequisite.

Selling is a dynamic process. New approaches will always be necessary, not least because markets are themselves dynamic and customer attitudes always changing. If this book forms a useful part of that ongoing search for effective approaches in selling, the time taken in writing it will have been worth while.

Preface

A moment's insight is sometimes worth a life's experience.
Oliver Wendell Holmes

My first job was in publishing. Indeed, it could be said that writing books is, in part, a kind of revenge for finally having to leave the business to try to earn sufficient money to buy my first house. However, it was an interesting time, and publishing is a unique and fascinating trade with which I have never lost touch.

Perhaps more relevant, it also introduced me to sales.

I made my first sales call on a small bookshop near Piccadilly, now long gone, and came away with an order; a fact that had more to do with the excellence of the list of titles I was describing than to any inherent sales skill I possessed at that stage of my career. Any sales briefing – training would be too grand a word – in those days consisted of being given some 'product information', a swatch of covers for forthcoming titles, and being told not to overdo the expenses. In past years many industries were little different.

Slowly, as I moved on in my career, I not only got more involved in sales, but also became more aware of the structure, skills and techniques which help make it effective. For most of my career, certainly in the last twenty or so years working in sales and marketing consultancy and training, I have been involved with a variety of companies, and have had the opportunity to observe and, I hope, assist their salespeople in what they do. Such work has been in a variety of industries and in a number of different countries.

It has been said that selling was never easy and that, in today's competitive market conditions, it is now downright difficult. Many in selling would agree. This book comes as a direct result of the sales process becoming more and more competitive. Selling has always involved good customer relations. Indeed, in the past, this has even been believed to be sufficient in itself. Selling has always demanded the application of techniques to make it persuasive, and certainly the two together – a persuasive approach and good customer relations – have led many sales people to success.

Both these skills are still needed today; the difference is that in today's competitive markets, however good the product or service being sold, they may still not be enough to ensure success. Something extra is needed. Selling has become an increasingly fragile process. All may be going well, and then one seemingly small factor, perhaps handled in an ill-prepared or inadequate fashion, makes a 'no' more likely. By contrast, a precision in everything that is done can invest elements of the sales process with the power to edge the customer towards 'yes'.

The salesperson who handles what they do in a way which recognises this fragility, and who understands and deploys appropriately the basic techniques – which remain important – gives themselves an edge in the market. An edge against competition which increases the likelihood of people wanting to do business with them.

Such an edge is available only to those salespeople who take a conscious view of the detail of what they do; selling cannot be carried out either 'by rote' or on automatic pilot. The born salesperson is, in my experience, a rare animal. The salespeople who make it look easy are, almost without exception, those who do prepare, think about what they do, and get the detail right.

Make no mistake, when I used the word 'fragile' of the sales process earlier, it was carefully chosen. Those things that make the difference may take a few seconds, perhaps they may represent a few sentences of a long conversation, or they may rest on one word. They are always important. For the most part there are no second prizes in selling. The order is either won or lost. So the details certainly matter.

This book therefore reviews the sales process in this light. It is not simply a restatement of the basic techniques, though these are reviewed. Rather, it focuses on those things within the structure of selling that make the difference between 'no' and 'yes'. We will be primarily concerned with business-to-business selling (industrial rather than consumer), though many of the principles and points made will have more general relevance. It is primarily for the salesperson (see *Note*, below), but will also be relevant to managers who have a sales role themselves, and sales managers and trainers who have the task of ensuring sales effectiveness in others.

This book is based on observation and experience. It does not try to lay down the law in terms of the 'right' way to sell. Rather, it sets out a way of thinking about, and thus approaching, selling, which is intended to allow a more sensitive and accurate deployment of the selling skills in a way that increases the chances of success. It relates only what seems to be 'best current practice'.

The final element in sales success will always be not just what is done, nor even how it is done, but the precise way in which an individual salesperson works, meeting by meeting, customer by customer, to make the sales techniques effective for them.

Patrick Forsyth
Touchstone Training & Consultancy
17 Clocktower Mews
London N1 7BB

(*Note* Words like 'salesman' seem to cause certain problems. Half the population may find them inappropriate. I have primarily used the word salesperson here, therefore, to describe the field salesman or representative, rather than in the wider interpretation of everyone in selling. A shop assistant might well be a salesperson, but that is not the kind of selling this book is primarily about. Similarly, until the English language comes up with a word meaning 'he or she' to everyone's satisfaction, no offence is intended to the many women now in selling by the unavoidable use of 'he' to include both.)

1

The Difference Between 'Yes' and 'No'

Unless one is a genius, it is best to
aim at being intelligible.
Anthony Hope

Selling, as we said in the Preface, was never easy and, in today's competitive market conditions, it can be downright difficult. It is also a fragile process. Both of these facts, and additionally the value of what is usually hanging on the outcome, means that it is too important to be allowed to go by default.

Yet, if what is done is ill-thought through or poorly carried out, this is exactly what will happen. Similarly, success is not guaranteed by any one factor and fine differences can be involved in making sure an order is secured. Both these facts are so important – indeed the way the selling task is reviewed throughout the book is based on it – that it is worth making clear by example before we proceed further. The following examples are all based on actual incidents, some that could happen all too often and all too easily. They illustrate moments during interviews that were otherwise going well, conducted by salespeople who, by any standard, would be called professional.

George is well into a meeting with an industrial buyer. All is going well. There is clear interest, the product has been well described and the buyer is seeking information about the cost-benefits of introducing the product into his production process. George knows this needs clarifying. He has not only planned how to deal with it, he has tailor-made two graphs to illustrate the financial justification and help clarify what can be a difficult area of explanation because of its complexities. He tells the buyer what he wishes to show him, and explains how it will help. He reaches into his briefcase and – after an embarrassing few minutes of not being able to locate the graphs – has to proceed without them. He does so pretty well in the circumstances – he is a good salesman – but the credibility of what he is doing is visibly diluted. The buyer, previously impressed, now has questions about efficiency, and service, in his mind. A week after the specifications and quotation are submitted, a letter arrives at George's office saying 'No, thank you'.

John has worked long and hard to get a hearing with a major industrial group. Several meetings with different people have cumulated in the opportunity to set out his company's range of services to the person he has identified as the key decision-maker. With the introductions over, he begins to set the scene and to lay out an overall picture of the services his company provides. 'We have a fragmented range of services,' he begins. The director says nothing, but his face and his mind say 'Fragmented?'. It is not simply the wrong word, it gives the opposite impression to that intended – a divisionalised structure to focus expertise in the different areas important to customers. At the crucial stage of an otherwise good interview, impact is diluted just when a sound first impression should have been made.

Discussions, subsequently, go no further.

Mary works for an organisation in financial services. She has had a number of meetings with one potential client, regarding pension schemes. Time has been spent obtaining information from them. Now armed with the many and complex details of what their situation and needs are, she is explaining her organisation's specific suggestions to the financial director. She starts to go through the details. Ten minutes later he interrupts, 'I have to say, I am really not following this at all.'

At least he is being honest; many a potential client would perhaps have said nothing. Until afterwards.

Even given the opportunity to recover, Mary finds no good reception to her subsequent follow ups after the meeting, and finally turns her attention, reluctantly, to others.

Peter receives a message to return a call to an important current prospect. He has had meetings with them, demonstrated equipment to them and, latterly, put in detailed specifications, proposals and costs for a tailor-made system. He knows he is now on a short-list of two potential suppliers. He makes the call optimistically, hoping a decision may have been made. They are still assessing the proposals he is told, and have a question about his. They turn together to the appropriate page and the prospect asks if a particular paragraph is, in fact, saying that one of the key technical criteria can be met. It is, and can be, and Peter says so, noticing as he does so that the wording of that paragraph is simply not quite clear. However, he reassures them and puts the telephone down.

A few days later the letter arrives. 'We are impressed by the technical solutions put forward in your proposals, but . . .'

Robert is a good salesman. He is technically expert – and able to explain his products and systems to people clearly – no mean achievement in the world of computer systems where jargon tends to outweigh clarity. But he is simply not so good on his feet. In formal presentations – a necessity in his business – his understanding of customers' needs and his ability with the technicalities are diluted by a hesitancy which detracts from what he is doing. It is not, in a sense, his fault. He has had no training, and has little experience in this area. But his customers make no allowance for this. Why should they? They are apt to equate presentational excellence, or lack of it, with technical excellence. This regularly gives his competitors an edge, if only on projects where formal presentation is necessary.

However, his success rate is lower than it might be.

In all these cases, and doubtless in many more occurring in meetings every day, the faults are not necessarily large ones. It is not that most of the necessary skills are not being deployed, nor even that the salespeople in question are not successful; indeed, most of the time they are.

Consider what went wrong in our examples: a forgotten detail of preparation (George's graphs); an ill-chosen word, and insufficient consciousness of what he was doing to correct it (John's opening); inadequate attention to clarity and perhaps, as a result, to benefits also (Mary's explanation); poor phraseology in a written proposal (Peter's document query); a blind spot, in an area made necessary by changing customer attitudes (Robert's presentation skills weakness).

The common factor with all these is that the areas of weakness are significant, perhaps crucial, to the success of the whole. Such slips may be sufficient to lose an order, or a customer. The effect is cumulative with any weaknesses adding together to give an overall poor impression to a customer. Imagine all the above faults being made by one salesperson in front of one customer. It is unlikely, in such a circumstance, that any order would result.

We must not imagine, however, that all such influences are negative. It is perfectly possible to balance such bad examples with good ones. Here are a couple, focusing on different factors to those illustrated above.

> **Brian** sells street sweepers, the small vehicles equipped with brushes and a giant 'hoover' which can be used to clean any area. He has organised a demonstration (as has one of his competitors) to a local authority. A group of council officers and employees are watching the machine go through its paces on a local shopping precinct. Brian is explaining as the demonstration proceeds, at one point mentioning the additional productivity possible with a two-man team. 'Let me show you,' he says, 'watch.' So saying he goes over to the machine and, taking a hoe off a rack at the back, he walks ahead and loosens a clump of weeds in its path. The machine negotiates the area leaving only a cloud of dust in its wake as Brian puts back the hoe.

Later, the chairman of the council is discussing the comparison between the two demonstrations, the machine in question and the service back-up that comes with them. They both do an excellent job. The chairman reminds his colleagues of Brian's action, 'I like a man who is prepared to get his hands dirty,' he says. 'I think we can rely on their service.'

After the next finance committee meeting, Brian duly gets his order.

Gill sells the accommodation and meeting space for an hotel. It is a nice hotel, and the facilities and service are good. But, for many meeting organisers, it is not so dissimilar to many others. Gill realises that, despite her view of the excellence of the property (after all she is exposed to it every day), customers and prospects forget quickly. But once people have been to the hotel, certainly if they have used it, it should be possible to remind them of it, and persuade them to use it again.

She constructs a follow-up system. By simply keeping a record of who she wants to remind, and establishing a frequency of contact – whether she writes, telephones, or sends them something (a newsletter, new brochure or postcard) – she makes sure that neither she, nor the hotel she sells, are forgotten. In an industry where this is not so usual, she stands out. Every few months those on the list get a contact, as the system is reliable and creatively implemented on a continuous basis.

Memories are successfully jogged, simply and cost-effectively.

As a result, the hotel does just that much more business than would otherwise be the case.

Again these examples illustrate small details: Brian joining the demonstration personally to make a particular point to his prospects; Gill working at a systematic approach to keep up ongoing contact. They may seem simple, and are certainly no more than common sense, but it, or its equivalent, does not always happen and sales may well be lost as a result.

Add these kinds of details, and once more the effect is cumulative, and the salespeople in question give themselves a positive edge. Given familiarity with the basics of sales technique, there is no limit to the number of such factors which can be deployed. There are, however, some areas of the sales process where getting the right approach is particularly important, real 'edge-givers' if you like. These will be identified as this book proceeds.

The foregoing examples are intended to establish more than simply the fragility of the sales process. What matters is what needs to happen to make it successful. It is, of course, impossible to tie this down to one simple factor. If this had ever been done it would no doubt have been patented and sold, making both great profit and books such as this one redundant. There are, however, underlying principles which act as foundations to success. We will now look at two principles which are of particular importance and use.

The first is the structure of the sales process. Selling is two-way, persuasive communication. Perhaps the best, simple definition of it is that selling is helping people to buy. It is not something we *do* to people, certainly not in isolation. Most salespeople are not in the business of selling, say, refrigerators; to reluctant Eskimos. (Actually Eskimos *do* buy refrigerators to enable them to keep food *warm* enough to cook without defrosting, but we digress.) Selling demands an understanding of how people make buying decisions; if what the salesperson does is based on that thinking process, then we have the right kind of basis on which to structure selling. We will look at these two processes alongside each other in just a moment.

The second principle, which separates the more from the less successful salespeople, is, quite simply, a consciousness of the structure and process, and the ability to fine-tune what is being done as the process progresses. There are entire libraries of books about developing a positive mental attitude, and the like, but *thinking* positive is not, in itself, sufficient. It is how this is done that allows the confidence to add constructively to sales technique. Imagine a tightrope walker. He pauses halfway across, and high above, the circus ring. If he allows himself to wonder whether he can complete his walk, it may well be in jeopardy. But he must not just remain confident, he must constantly apply all his underlying experience, skill and understanding of what he is doing to allow him to complete the walk safely. He may have to adjust what he is doing, constantly shifting his grip, perhaps, on the long pole he carries for balance, adjusting to the tension of the high-wire and the movement of his fellow artistes. So, in selling, the salesperson must adjust, constantly, and be ever vigilant of how things are going. The salesperson, too, relies on his underlying understanding of the principles and structure of sales technique to help him with the constant and necessary adjustment.

This is a little different from an appeal for a positive mental attitude. Indeed, it is a practical skill which can be developed and practised. In some respects it is rightly said that 'selling gets worse with practice', meaning that because customers are not on our side, salespeople tend to react protectively to any rejection or lack of interest. They adjust what they do in a way which, while avoiding confrontation, may dilute their effectiveness. This happens very clearly in closing. Saying 'Will you buy?' is dangerous; customers may say 'No' (and in some cases they may say it rather less than politely). Saying 'Is that all the information you need for the moment?' allows the customer to respond pleasantly, 'Yes, that's fine, thank you very much', but negatively. The net effect is 'Leave it with me'. You can no doubt think of other examples.

A similar effect occurs through sheer boredom. Any salesperson making five or six calls a day will be making well over a thousand a year. It frankly gets tedious to repeat the same message many times and, while everything needs tailoring to individual customers' needs, it is easy to alter elements which should be the same in a way that dilutes sales effectiveness.

In a competitive market place, the fact that some salespeople will be making mistakes and that prevailing standards are not universally excellent, means that it may only need an attention to detail for your approach to stand out positively to buyers and increase your chances of success. This makes for a major opportunity for those prepared to take the trouble to get it right!

Reviewing the process is perhaps an example of taking just that sort of trouble. So how will *we* review the process as we move on?

The following chapters follow the broad chronology of what typically happens in the sales process. Chapter 2 looks at the important topic of setting up meetings, who you should see and how you make contact. Such initial contact is usually by letter or telephone; telephone contact will be dealt with in some detail, and a link made with the comment on written communication that appears in Chapter 6. Then, in Chapter 3, we look at preparation; an under-rated preliminary to selling that can make a major difference to the chances of success. This is followed, in Chapter 4, by a review of the structure of the sales process and the manner in which techniques should be deployed.

Chapter 5, the longest in the book, reviews the whole sequence of what happens during the face-to-face meeting, and Chapter 6 looks at the written proposals and formal presentations which will often be required whenever the customer cannot confirm a purchase at the first meeting. These follow-up activities must be every bit as persuasive as the face-to-face contact.

Next, in Chapter 7, we look at the need for and techniques of further follow up, the tactics that will tie down the first order and develop an account into one you do business with regularly. This is followed by consideration of the issues affecting the way in which major sales are handled, on the basis that large customers are different in nature as well as scale and therefore need special attention. The final chapter summarises and recaps the key issues, and the Afterword looks ahead at how the sales job is developing, and is likely to develop in future.

Those points that will have a disproportionate influence on the outcome – that make the difference between 'Yes' and 'No' – are highlighted at various points throughout the text in boxed sections. Each of these is individually significant, but their overall impact, it should be borne in mind, is cumulative. These points all reinforce each other and create a real overall 'edge'.

2

First Contact – *setting up, getting in*

> I am a great believer in luck, and I find the
> harder I work the more I have of it.
> *Stephen Leacock*

Before you can sell, effectively or otherwise, you need someone to sell to – a prospect. Creating prospects is not the easiest part of selling, nor is getting in to see them. One of many apocryphal stories about salespeople concerns the salesman who tells of finally arriving at a meeting arranged with a prospect he found very difficult to get to see. 'You should feel honoured,' says the prospect, 'I have refused appointments with twelve salesmen like you already this week.' 'I know,' replies the salesman. 'I'm them!'

If you only sell to established customers, if prospecting is no part of what you do, then you may consider skipping this chapter. But most businesses are dependent, to some degree, on new customers, and prospecting is therefore an important part of what most salespeople do.

Prospecting should always start with planning. Planning seems tedious. Planning seems boring and is, perhaps, the least interesting aspect of selling. Worse, planning may seem unnecessary. After all, the best salespeople make it look so easy. The truth is very much the opposite. Magic formulae, or rather the lack of them, have been referred to earlier, but planning can almost be regarded as a hidden magic formula. In my experience, after observing the many salespeople I have met and worked with, the most successful are those who do worry about planning.

Planning works. It makes it more likely that you will do business at the end of the day.

At this stage it is worth noting that planning is a key factor, one we will return to as we continue through the book.

There are only, at base, four factors which dictate success in selling. They are:

who you see – you must select the right people, the best prospects and not waste time on those who are unlikely ever to buy;

how many you see – productivity is important, the more well-selected people you see (without sacrificing the quality of meeting held with them) the more likely it is that sales targets are to be met;

SALES EDGE 1 | Planning

- the first rule is 'Do it'
- plan who to see
- plan how to get to see them
- plan your time
- plan ongoing relationships

Planning increases the likelihood of people doing business with you. It takes a little time, often not too much, but it is worth while. All other things being equal, planning gives the well-prepared salesperson an edge. It allows you to relate better to the customer, and to differentiate yourself from competition. Without it you may find you regularly leave meetings thinking 'If only . . .'

Plan the work and work the plan

---

how often you see them – the frequency of ongoing contact must be appropriate, you need to see people with sufficient regularity, one appropriate to the relationship it is intended to build with them.

These first three factors all relate to planning; the fourth

what you do when you get there – of course, concerns the whole area of the quality of sales approach. This is an important area, but one which is influenced in turn by the first three.

The first three factors are planning matters. You must select the right people, the best prospects; you must be productive and see as many people as possible (without sacrificing the quality of meeting); and you must see them with the right frequency and follow up. The fourth factor, of course, concerns the whole area of the quality of sales approach. This is an important area, but one influenced in turn by the first three.

Sales Productivity

Sales productivity can be assessed using a 'work study'. Doing so provides a basis for all sales activity and ensures that prospecting can not only be fitted in, but also gets an appropriate amount of time.

Such a calculation ensures that the amount of work attempted is realistic. If it is not, either valuable and expensive time will be wasted, or profitable opportunities will be lost. All you need to do is the following.

1. Count the number of existing and potential customers you intend to visit during the year.
2. Assign to each customer a call frequency – the number of calls you believe will be sufficient to gain or keep the identified business in the account.
3. Calculate the annual number of working days in the field – excluding holidays, sales meetings, training courses, exhibitions etc. Normally this will not total much more than between 200 to about 220 days.

4. Calculate the average number of calls made on each day in the field.

5. Substitute the above figures to this formula:

$$\text{Workload} = \frac{\text{No. of customers/potential customers} \times \text{Annual call frequency}}{\text{Average daily call rate} \times \text{No. of working days per year}}$$

The perfect workload should be 1.00. That is to say, the number of calls you intend to make should balance with the number of calls you can make. However, since we are not dealing with very precise data, there should be little cause for concern if the workload varies between 0.90 and 1.10.

If the above calculation shows that your workload is too heavy, the following questions should be considered.

1. Are all the customers equally important? Is there any other way of servicing the less important ones: through distributors, or internal staff, for instance.
2. Are all the call frequencies the minimum necessary to win and hold the business? Could adequate contact be maintained with fewer visits and better use of the telephone?
3. Is the average daily call rate the best that can be achieved?

After answering these questions a balance should be struck which will be realistic. For some this may mean discussion with sales management. Such a calculation acknowledges that time is one of your most valuable commodities, indeed it may well be that every time you make a call the total cost may well be up to £100, or more in some industries. This is a good deal of money just to say 'Good morning' if planning has not been worked out sensibly.

With a view of productivity of this sort in mind, we will now turn to the new customers who will form part of the mix. The following questions form a checklist approach to selecting and approaching customers, or prospects as they are at this stage.

Why should customers do business with you?

The answer to this question starts with an analysis of why your existing customers do business with you. What product/service advantages do you have? What is it about your organisation that they like? This will include both broad statements – 'We provide excellent quality at a good price' – and detail – 'We offer personalised customer back-up service, through a dedicated technical person'. It may also be useful to have in mind some negative factors – 'They have to be happy to wait for our six to eight weeks' delivery time'.

What kind of customer is most likely to be a prospect?

This question needs approaching in three areas:

the customer type;
the customer situation;
the buyer.

In other words, you need to ask what kind of customer, e.g. size, industry etc.; what situation of customer, e.g. growth companies, one with high-priced products; and who is the decision-maker, e.g. the buyer, the finance director; all contribute to the focus you can then put on the kind of prospect you will go after.

What do you, ideally, need to know about them?

You will need to know about their structure, organisation, kind of business and so on. Information on this, and more, can be invaluable. When we come to Figure 1 in Chapter 3, we will see that it provides an example of the kind of approach (one for which you may feel a tailored checklist is useful) that looks at these factors comprehensively. An additional consideration is how much of this can be found out in advance; some research with trade directories or other sources may be worth while.

How do you select priorities?

In a word, practically. Existing customers are easiest to sell to; past or dormant customers (who do know, and hopefully like, your organisation from the past) are next; leads, enquiries from such as direct mail shots are next; and cold prospects are the most difficult. The questions already posed will help focus what must be done cold on those who are most likely to be suitable, and it is almost always better to focus than to adopt a shotgun approach.

How do you approach your prospects?

There are three options, namely, a letter, a telephone call or a combination of the two, a letter followed by a telephone call, for instance. Simply knocking on their door, the ultimate 'cold call' is likely to bring the smallest conversion, but it could be relevant for some (it has been used successfully in areas as diverse as office cleaning and business equipment for example) and in certain respects it is productive – working systematically through an industrial estate or office block, for instance.

The principles of letter-writing are not dissimilar to those applicable to any other kind of written communication, and these are reviewed later in Chapter 6. The appointment-making telephone call will be dealt with in this chapter, while investigating the peculiarities of telephone technique is covered in an appendix at the end of the chapter in order to keep that detail separate from the call itself.

What are your objectives in approaching them?

This may seem obvious, namely to sell them something. But what is the first contact for? To obtain information or to make an appointment? If the latter, when and where will that be? At their office or factory? At an exhibition or demonstration? You need to have all this clearly in mind before you lift the telephone.

When do you want to see them?

Not just 'as soon as possible', but at a time and date that suits your schedule and productivity. Beware of suspect 'stated wisdom', such as 'No buyer wants to see you before 10 a.m.' when in fact some will not only happily see you at 8.30 a.m., but you are likely to have an uninterrupted hour until their switchboard opens. Neither should you believe that 'No buyer will see you after 4 p.m. or on Fridays, or when there is an R in the month'.

In fact everyone's habits are different, and you simply risk restricting your opportunities if you make unwarranted assumptions.

With the answers to all the foregoing in mind it is now time to think about actually making an appointment. Ultimately, even if a letter has been sent, you will soon find yourself on the telephone. The telephone is a form of communication that presents both problems and opportunities. It is not everyone's favourite kind of call, but a structured approach helps. You still will not win them all, but you will get a better success rate; and if you do that, at every stage, you will sell more in the end. Before we speak to the prospect, however, there is still something else to consider.

Getting Through to the Right Person

This is not just a matter of defeating the mechanical gremlins of the telephone company, but being able to make direct contact with the decision-maker. This difficulty alone can get salespeople off to an uneasy start in prospecting. Switchboards and secretaries are often past masters at spotting, and refusing, anyone who is selling.

Some simple rules will help you overcome this problem.

In 'cold calling' prior research may have given you the name you want. If not, always ask for the name first and then ask to be put through, e.g.:

Salesman 'May I have the name of your chief accountant?'
Operator 'You mean Mr Morris?'

Then ask to speak to him. You may be put straight through and you will know as he answers 'Morris here' that you have the right person, avoiding the need to check who he is as he answers. Operators and secretaries will often put a call through to a department or assistant first rather than the manager himself.

Alternatively, more questioning may follow:

Operator 'Who is calling Mr Morris?'
Salesman 'Mr Roberts.'

At this stage you may be put through, particularly if you say your name confidently. The same applies to the question 'What company are you with?'. You should answer confidently and without volunteering any extra information.

The really protective switchboard operator will then ask 'What are you calling about?'. Avoid cliché and dishonest answer, e.g. 'a research survey', and describe briefly and comprehensively what you want to discuss (*not* what you want to sell), e.g. 'I need to talk to Mr Morris about computer stationery for the new EDP installations at your branches'. A secretary/operator is unlikely to want to get involved in the detail of what may by then sound a little complicated and you should, at this point, get through.

For regular or follow-up contacts the same principles apply, at least if there remains a chance your prospect would rather not speak to you. It is useful to refer back to past events, e.g. 'I agreed with Mr Morris when I saw him last month that I would call this week'. Only phrase it this way if it *was* agreed; alternatively say 'I said to Mr Morris . . .' or, having written suggesting you call him on a particular day, 'Mr Morris is expecting to hear from me today'. (This kind of approach can also be used as a follow up to the right kind of phrase in a selling/prospecting letter.)

If the buyer is not at the office, the secretary may offer to help or take a message. The most useful piece of information you can obtain is when the contact will be available to take a call. Ask 'May I call back this afternoon?' or 'Will he be available tomorrow morning?'. This saves you time in further wasted calls and means that you can tell the operator next time, 'I arranged with Mr Morris's secretary to call him at about this time'.

Whatever kind of call you are making it is necessary to get through to the right person; what follows depends on the nature of the call and your objectives.

Making the Appointment

Whoever you are calling, whether it is someone who has seen a brochure, responded to an advertisement or mail shot, or simply a 'cold prospect', think about the call before you make it.

Before you even dial the prospect's number, you must have at hand the following:

- all customer information available to date, including any 'personal hints', which can help avoid simple gaffes such as the wrong pronunciation of someone's name;
- information on your availability for appointments;
- a checklist of the information you ideally want – other services being used by the customer, their preferences, size of company, or whatever is relevant.

Once you are through to the right person (see p. 15) – and this is worth checking, particularly if you have been transferred more than once – you need a structured approach to give you the best chance of success.

There are seven key stages to follow (some taking only a few seconds) when making the majority of such calls.

1. A greeting

Greetings should be kept short, simple and to the point. It may be no more than 'Good morning', and can link to check that you have a successful connection, 'Is that John Robertson?'.

2. Identification

Any identification should be clear and, allowing how bad many people are at retaining a name, may contain an element of repetition, 'My name is Forsyth, Patrick Forsyth, from Touchstone Training & Consultancy'. Then, allowing for any response, move promptly into the next stage.

3. Reason for calling

Your reason that you give for calling must be customer-oriented, containing a benefit, and explaining why you want an *appointment* (do not try to sell the whole product/service at this stage), perhaps mentioning something the customer will be able to see, touch, try out or have demonstrated at the meeting, something which can only take place at a meeting.

It helps to speak of the meeting as 'working with the customer' (rather than 'doing something to them'), for instance 'when we meet we can go through the details together and make sure we come to the right solution'. This creates a feeling of customer orientation.

4. Request for appointment

There is no substitute for asking for an appointment. However, bear in mind the following.

- Mention the duration of the meeting. Honestly. It is no good pretending you only need 30 minutes if you need an hour. At worst you may arrive and find they have only exactly the 30 minutes you asked for on the telephone.
- Give the customer a reasonable lead time. They are less likely to refuse an appointment for 7–10 days' time than to refuse an appointment for tomorrow.
- Offer an alternative. 'Would 3.00 p.m. Thursday afternoon be suitable, or would you prefer a morning, say Wednesday morning?' State the first option more precisely than the second.

5. Respond to objections

Now and again resistance will be met, but you can then employ an objection-handling technique called the 'boomerang' technique. This is particularly useful for 'turning' an objection to your advantage. For instance:

Prospect 'It's not convenient – I haven't the time.'

Salesperson 'It's because I know you're busy that a short meeting may be useful. It will give you the opportunity to hear how we go about things and see whether scheduling more time to discuss the project is worth while.'

When you have got them back on track again, and sounding even tentatively agreeable, you can 'close' again as fast as is polite – with the appointment as your objective.

If it is impossible to make an appointment, you can still get something from the situation by getting some new information for the records. Having 'won' the conversation and 'negotiation' to that point, prospects will often be in the frame of mind to allow you some concessions, and may be quite willing to give you information about future plans, changes or the names of others in the organisation you could contact, etc.

Further examples of objection handling can be seen, if we look at the four different types of objections you may encounter.

The unspoken objection

This is difficult to overcome. It is there, real enough, in the prospect's mind, but is unspoken. Without any feedback other than voice (a puzzled look is not visible over the telephone), you must literally 'read between the lines' to discover when this is happening. If you believe it is then you should ask questions and encourage the prospect to raise whatever is on their mind. This works even to the point of suggesting hesitation: 'I detect a slight hesitation, are you sure Friday is OK? I could equally well do one day next week'; or 'You don't sound sure, I do want to make sure the time is convenient for you; does it really suit?'.

The legitimate objection

This is a genuine reason for a prospect's lack of interest. But, it may be short-lived, the need may arise later or someone else in the organisation might respond positively. If so, the following approaches would be relevant:

[Prospect]	[Salesperson]
I'm right in the middle of the budget preparation. I can't see anyone right now.'	'I understand, Mrs Smith. When would be a better time for me to call you back?'
'Thanks for calling, but that kind of decision is outside my authority. It would be a waste of time for us to meet.'	'OK, thanks for that, Mr Black. May I ask who I should contact? Can I say you referred me to them?'
'Look, before you go any further, I can't see us needing your product. We bought something similar a few months ago and, unless there's a remarkable growth in the market, we're fully equipped for the foreseeable future.'	'Ah I see. Then clearly a meeting now would seem unproductive. I wonder if, rather than us meeting now, you could give me some background information over the phone . . . Thank you very much, Mr Cooper. I'd like to call you again in 3 months when the growth you spoke about may well have happened.'

One other form of legitimate objection is a complaint about a minor, but real, product disadvantage; a perceived, but incorrect, product limitation; or a negative past relationship. In all these cases the response should be the same:

a) *accept* the prospect's point of view without necessarily agreeing with it;

b) *minimise* or correct the point of view by repeating the objection in your own words in the form of a question, and playing down its real or perceived impact;

c) *compensate* by referring to one or more definite advantages which outweigh the small disadvantage.

The false objection

A false objection is the prospect's argument or excuse for not granting an appointment for a face-to-face interview. As the name implies, it is not the real reason for avoiding a meeting. For example:

'Your product/company just isn't any good'	He or she is hiding a true objection: what is it that makes the target say this?
'I'm not interested'	He or she needs more information to become interested
'Your prices are too high'	The real meaning here is that the desire for the product is too low

To overcome these objections you must ask questions and get the prospect to reveal his or her true objection to meeting with you. For example, if – and this is a common one – the point is made that prices are too high, you might say, 'Of course, it is a substantial amount of money, but when you say that, what are you comparing it with?'; this to focus the conversation on the real feelings.

'Classic' telephone objections

Prospects frequently state an objection rather than put the phone down on a sales caller. Such objections sometimes have a grain of truth in them but often they are used as part of a game that prospects play to test your resolve and persistence, or your

21

professionalism (are you reading a telescript?) or give the impression that they are less available for an interview than may actually be the case.

The tone of their voice, persistence of objection or conviction in their own objection will tell you whether an objection is of this nature. The quicker a prospect positively responds to and accepts your reply to an objection, the more likely it is that it will have been this sort. For example:

[Prospect]	**[Salesperson]**
'You're just trying to sell me something.'	'No. It's too early to say that! First we must explore your needs and see what sort of benefits from my product you consider important.'
'You'll be wasting your time giving me a sales pitch.'	'That's one thing I won't do. What I would like to do is discuss how we can help increase your productivity and improve your sales. I'm sure our time wouldn't be wasted.'
'Look, just give me a quick description and tell me what it costs.'	'Well, I could do that but I don't believe it would be fair to you. As we offer a wide range of models and prices I can't recommend the right one for you until I understand your requirements. You could give me a feel for these at a short meeting at which I can show you how easy it is to install any of our models and get their immediate and significant benefits.'

6. Ask questions

While questions are not always necessary, some may be a pre-requisite to a good meeting, helping with planning and making sure you are 'on target' once you are face-to-face with your prospect.

A checklist of questions that may be necessary in your business will be invaluable.

One hint, which can often be overlooked, is that if you are visiting the prospect (which they may prefer, particularly for a first meeting) do ask about location. A sentence or two may save you hours of searching. What about parking? Is there a car park?

Similarly, if the prospects are visiting your office make sure they know exactly how to find your premises; confirm this in writing (with a map if you have one) and remember to inform others at your office (including the receptionist) as necessary, making sure they know how important the visit is to the firm.

7. Thanks and confirmation

At this stage you should summarise briefly what will now happen, 'Right, I will put that brochure in the post to you, Mr Black, and look forward to seeing you, at your office, at 3.00 p.m. on Monday 27 July.' No more may be required at this stage, though sometimes it is also appropriate to organise written confirmation.

Ringing the prospect to make an appointment can be an awkward kind of call to make: you may well be conscious of the degree of 'push' involved, but a systematic approach will make it easier for you to conduct the call and make it acceptable at the other end.

What next? Well, if we are optimistic, we will assume that the prospect says 'yes' to a meeting, so the next thing is to *plan* the meeting.

Postscript to Chapter 2: The Ubiquitous Telephone

Any telephone conversation is simply two-way communication, albeit using a particular medium. It is surely not difficult, after all some people talk on the phone socially for hours and hours. On the other hand, like any communication, there may be a good deal hanging on it. Any problem will dilute the chances of success. And the problems of 'voice-only' communication are considerable, and in some cases prohibitive. It pays therefore to consider all the factors that can make vocal communication successful, and not underrate it as 'simply a telephone call'.

It is important to look at how you use the telephone itself; your voice and manner; obtaining and using feedback; and planning. The telephone distorts the voice, exaggerating the rate of your speech and heightening the tone. You must talk into the mouthpiece in a clear, normal voice (if you are a woman, it can help to pitch the voice lower). It is surprising how many things can interfere with the simple process of talking directly into the mouthpiece: smoking; eating; trying to write; holding a file or book open at the correct page and holding the phone; sorting through the correct change in a call box; allowing others in the room to interrupt or allowing a bad-quality line to disrupt communication (it is better to phone back). These points are all quite obvious, yet it is so easy to get them a little bit wrong, thus reducing the effectiveness of your communication.

Voice and manner

Remember that on the phone you only have your voice and manner to rely on in making an impression. None of the other factors of personality are perceptible. Here are some suggestions that may help you to make a good impact.

Speak at a slightly slower rate than usual
Speaking too rapidly makes it easier to be misunderstood and also mistrusted, although, by contrast, speaking too slowly can make the listener impatient or irritated.

Smile. Use a warm tone of voice
Though a smile cannot be seen, it does change the tone of your voice. Make sure you sound pleasant, efficient and, perhaps most important, interested and enthusiastic about the conversation. You will find that enthusiasm is contagious.

Get the emphasis right
Make sure that you emphasise the parts of the communication that are important to the listener or for clarity. Only your voice can give the emphasis you want.

Ensure clarity
Make sure you are heard, especially with names, numbers, etc. It is easy to confuse S's and F's for instance or find that 15 per cent is taken to mean 50 per cent.

Be positive
Have the courage of your convictions. Do not say 'possibly', 'maybe', 'I think' or 'that could be' (watch this one, or you could give out a circumspect feeling).

Be concise
Ensure a continuous flow of information, but in short sentences, a logical sequence and saying one thing at a time. Watch for and avoid the wordiness that creeps in when we need time to think, e.g. 'at this moment in time' (now), 'along the lines of' (like).

Avoid jargon
Whether the jargon is that of your own firm (e.g. abbreviated description of a department name), the industry (e.g. technical descriptions of processes), or general (e.g. phrases like 'I'll see to that immediately' – do you mean in 5 minutes or 5 hours?). At least check that the other person understands, they may not want to risk losing face by admitting that you are being too technical for them, and a puzzled look will not be visible. Jargon can too easily become a prop to self-confidence.

Be descriptive

The only picture people will have in their minds will be the one you put there. Anything – such as saying 'it makes programming your video recorder seem straightforward' – that conjures up images in the mind of the listener will stimulate additional response from someone restricted to the single stimulus of voice.

Use gestures

Your style will come across differently depending on your physical position. For example, there may even be certain kinds of call that you can make better standing up rather than sitting down, debt collecting or laying down the law perhaps. (Really! Try it; it works).

Get the right tone

Be friendly without being flippant. Be efficient, courteous, whatever is called for in the circumstances.

Be natural

Be yourself. Avoid adopting a separate, contrived telephone 'persona'. Consider the impression you want to give: Do you want to sound mature, expert, authoritative, for example?

Your intention is to prompt the other person into action. You should speak naturally in a way that is absolutely clear. Here are some useful additional rules.

Be courteous

Always be courteous.

Be efficient

Project the right image.

Be personal

Use 'I' and say what you will do.

Be appreciative

'Thank you' is a good phrase (but do not be gushing).

Obtaining and using feedback

Talk *with* people, not at them

As a first step to encouraging a response, form a picture of your listener (or imagine them if you know them) and use this to remove the feeling of talking to a disembodied voice.

Remember to listen

Don't talk all the time. You cannot talk and listen simultaneously.

Clarify as you proceed

Ask questions, check back as you go along – it may appear impolite to ask later.

Take written notes

Note down anything, everything, that might be useful later in the conversation or at subsequent meetings. Get the whole picture and avoid the prospect saying 'but I said that earlier', which can indicate that your credibility is suffering. And do it as you proceed, not at the end of the call.

Maintain a two-way flow

Do not interrupt, let your prospect finish each point, but make sure, if they are talking at some length, that they know you are listening. Say 'Yes' or 'That's right' to show you are still there.

Concentrate

Shut out all distractions, interruptions and 'noises off'. It may be apparent to your listener if you are not concentrating on him or her alone – it will appear as lack of interest.

Do not overreact

It is easy to jump to conclusions or make assumptions about a person you cannot see – resist this temptation.

'Read between the lines'

Do not just listen to what is said but also what is meant. Make sure you catch any nuance and observe every reaction to what you are saying.

Planning

Because we are attempting to gain agreement or commitment, planning the call beforehand is important.

I do not mean a lengthy period of preparation, though certain calls may be well worth planning more formally, but it does mean that the brain must always start working before the mouth opens! Making a few notes and a few moments' thought before dialling is usually well worth while. This kind of planning will help you:

– overcome tension or nervousness;
– improve your ability to think fast enough;
– prevent side-tracking (or being side-tracked);
– make sure you talk from the listener's point of view;
– assess your own effectiveness.

And above all it will help you to set clear and specific objectives designed to gain agreement and commitment from the other person.

Planning is necessary even to cope with incoming calls (at least those that follow a pattern). If you have made plans you will be able to direct or control the conversation without losing flexibility, and react to others accurately, without being led on by them. Plan to make difficult calls early and do not put them off – they will not get easier, rather the reverse.

To repeat, never think of any call as 'just a phone call'.

How you sound

It is a good idea to know how you sound to a listener at the other end of the line.

This is not difficult to organise; a standard cassette recorder or dictating machine on which you can record your own voice is all that is necessary to stimulate what you would hear on the telephone.

Practise simply by talking and playing back. More usefully, rehearse any particularly important, or repeating, call which you know you have to make.

Better still, get a friend or colleague to hold a conversation with you so that you hear yourself, on playback, responding to questions and conversation that you were not expecting.

If you have not done this before it is likely that even a few minutes of self-analysis will show you a lot, and allow any specific weaknesses or habits to be improved.

3

Call Preparation – *giving yourself an (unfair) advantage*

Well begun is half done.
Proverb

Preparation is important. Now, before you turn over or skip this chapter, let us look at that remark in another way. Call preparation, the final elements of the planning process, can make the difference between getting an order or not. So it is worth a moment of your time. Simply put, it is the expedient of engaging the brain before opening the mouth. It is important enough to give it the status of an 'edge-giver' before we even explore it.

That said, how do we go about it? Planning is traditionally a weak area, and, if your competitors are not good at it, so much the better for you – if you are prepared it will differentiate you, or at least play a part in the process.

The first rule about preparing the call, each and every call, is therefore simple; you must do it. It is a necessary discipline – an attitude of mind, even – that prompts objective thinking about what *can* be achieved, what *must* be achieved, and *how* to deploy techniques and resources to maximise the likelihood of success.

As has already been said, successful salespeople, in any field, are usually those who do their homework. This may mean a few moments' thought sitting in the car just before you go in to see a prospect; a few minutes going through the files, perhaps the night before; or a couple of hours sitting round the table with colleagues to thrash out the best approach.

Such preparation allows you to ensure that the meeting will focus on the individual and that you are fluent and confident in what you do. It will also save time (a valuable resource for both parties), compared with a less well-prepared and well-structured meeting.

Because the circumstances in each case are different, we will review preparation for calls on existing customers and prospects separately.

SALES EDGE 2 | Preparing the Meeting

- the first rule is 'always do it'
- think ahead
- work out the structure and sequence
- set clear objectives
- anticipate reactions

Preparation creates a structure, a route map not a strait-jacket, which will guide you through the meeting. It will not, cannot, anticipate everything that will happen. It is certainly not intended to provide a script. Nor does it restrict your ability to operate, creatively, off the cuff where appropriate. It is designed to make being able to do so more straightforward and more likely to be effective.

Prepare well; it puts you in the driving seat

Existing Customers

Planning calls on your existing customers can be comparatively easy: relationships and documentation already exist, from which information can be drawn to create the basis of your call.

31

However, even though the relationship and the data in your files will give you a great advantage over a competing newcomer, it's important that you recognise the essentially *defensive* nature of selling to an existing customer (where you will be 'defending' your product and your relationship from competitor activity), compared to the essentially *offensive* nature of selling to a prospect (where you will be the one 'attacking' to win the prospect's business from their current supplier). Planning an effective defence against predators is as important as planning an attack on your competitors' customers.

There are nine main factors you should consider when planning a call on an existing customer.

The customer's buying record
What has been purchased, when, in what quantities and to what value? Look at the customer's payment record: are any invoices outstanding? Are you still liable for any returns (up-lifted, or sale or return stock)? Are the people involved in the customer's decision-making process (which may well involve several people) the same; are the policies the same; are the influences on purchase decisions the same? Think about the customer's current circumstances and plans: is their potential order a regular order to replenish stock (a straight repeat purchase), or might it be a modified repurchase (i.e. they want a product variant), or might it be a completely new purchase to satisfy their business development plans? What happened last time?

The overall objectives and resources
What are the product mix, volume, value and penetration targets for your territory? What are the available sales aids (for your use and those designed as leave-behinds for customers or end-users)? Is your call supported by advertising and/or merchandising? What are the campaign dates? Are you fully resourced: product knowledge, demonstration skills, literature, samples, record cards, forward appointments, business cards, etc.?

Call objectives
Do you have all the data needed to create maximum and fallback call objectives, objectives that are realistic and achievable?

The call opening
Do you know what to say, how to appear, how to behave in order to build on the existing relationship?

The interview
Which interview plan will you use? Have you worked out what questions to ask, and in what sequence? Have you ideas about the customer's needs, and thus how you will resolve them?

Possible objections
What might they be; when might they arise; how will you handle them?

The close
How will you close? (And, if negotiation – a whole additional area – is involved, what variables are you prepared to concede; which ones are fixed; what must you gain from any negotiation?)

Follow up
How will you build a link from this call to the next?

Time
With all that you must achieve with this customer at this call, have you worked out a personal time plan, designed to maximise your utilisation of the available working hours?

Clearly, the more facts you know about your existing customers' needs and habits, the more you should be able to answer these planning questions. However, be aware that such knowledge can lead to over-confidence, and could blind you to seeing opportunities that a newcomer, with a more inquisitive mind and 'attacking' stance, might spot. In other words, are you sure that you have the complete – and up-to-date – picture concerning every part of your customer's business where one of your products might fit?

Prospects

Obviously, a serious problem with prospects is often the lack of information available about them and, by definition, the lack of a relationship.

Your planning emphasis must therefore be on research and the actual interview opening, which is, it might be argued, more important to the success of a prospect visit than to an existing customer, because the opening moments of a prospect interview create a sharply-defined focus on which the chance of a future relationship depends.

Thus, the more relevant you can make your opening the higher will be your chances of raising your prospect's interest and receptiveness, and of building trust – the very necessary ingredient of empathy. Remember, you may not have more than one chance to get close to a prospect: your first approach, particularly if winning business from a competitor is the prize, must be a good one.

There are four main factors which constitute the research and planning demands for visits to prospects.

- **Desk research on the prospect's** financial status; his markets and customers; specifications; corporate objectives; owners, directors and other key stakeholders; strategic business units; products; processes; plant; employees; unions, etc. This information can be found in the prospect's annual or mid-term financial and shareholders' reports, in relevant business directories and reference books, and so on.

- **Face-to-face research on the prospect's** decision-makers and purchase influencers; buying patterns; current and future needs, etc.

- **Possible call objectives**. These should be detailed as the available pre-call data allows, but remember that your objectives will probably need revising on the spot in the light of your initial meeting.

- **Prospect development** or how to create and develop a relationship which benefits both parties. (You may only be able to plan this after your initial meeting.)

The checklists in Figure 3.1 will help you fill out these principles.

Figure 3.1 Call planning sales checklists

Existing customers	Yes	No

1. Are my *objectives:*
- stated as customer needs?
- commercially worth while?
- consistent with our policy?
- achievable within our resources?
- measurable?
- timed?

2. Have I done enough *research* on:
- the person to be seen?
- the customer situation?
- recommenders?
- influencers?
- supporters?
- their needs?
- competition?

3. Will my *opening:*
- put him at ease?
- get him interested and talking?
- explore his needs?
- establish his priorities?

4. Will my *presentation:*
- offer desirable results from his point of view?

	Yes	No
• prove my case to his satisfaction?	___	___
• explain complex points simply?	___	___
• show how his needs can be met?	___	___

5. If he raises *objections:*

	Yes	No
• have I considered what they might be?	___	___
• have I got answers which will satisfy him?	___	___
• are they related to his needs?	___	___

6. Will my *close:*

	Yes	No
• get a commitment?	___	___
• match my objectives?	___	___
• make it easy for him to agree?	___	___
• leave him feeling better than before the call?	___	___

7. In terms of *equipment:*

	Yes	No
• have I identified what I will need?	___	___
• have I identified what he may need?	___	___
• have I got it with me?	___	___
• have I decided how to use it?	___	___

Prospects

	Yes	No
1. For *objectives* see Checklist 1 on page 35.		
2. Have I done enough *research* on:		
• background information on this prospect?	___	___
– published sources?	___	___
– prospect sources?	___	___
– other sources?	___	___
• background information on his industry?	___	___
– published sources?	___	___
– prospect sources?	___	___
– other sources?	___	___
• background information on his competition?	___	___
– published sources?	___	___

- prospect sources?   ____   ____
- other sources?   ____   ____
- possible needs?   ____   ____
- major needs?   ____   ____
- future plans?   ____   ____
- whether there is an obvious need for my   ____   ____
  product/services?
- whether it has sales potential?   ____   ____

(and see Checklist 1)

3. Will my *opening:*
- fill gaps in essential knowledge?   ____   ____
  - buying process?   ____   ____
  - decision-makers?   ____   ____
  - industry situation?   ____   ____
  - company situation?   ____   ____
  - organisation?   ____   ____
  - needs?   ____   ____
  - competition?   ____   ____
    - his?   ____   ____
    - ours?   ____   ____
- impress him about me?   ____   ____
- impress him about the company?   ____   ____

(and see Checklist 1)

4. For *presentations* see Checklist 1.
5. For *objections* see Checklist 1.
6. For *close* see Checklist 1.
7. For *equipment* see Checklist 1.

None of this planning is of real use without clear objectives, however, the better the information you have, or have put together, the more precisely you can then set your objectives.

Setting Objectives

There is an old saying which advises 'if you don't know where you are going, any road will do'. So it is with objectives: if you know what the end point is it will help you work back and establish how to get there, how to open, how to tackle each stage.

A call objective must be concise, but nevertheless expressed in the five 'dimensions' represented by the familiar mnemonic **SMART** (**S**pecific **M**easurable **A**chievable **R**ealistic and **T**imed). That is, a call objective must be:

specific – expressed precisely;

measurable – it must contain a quantified goal against which your performance can be measured;

achievable – it must not be so difficult as to make its achievement beyond your current capabilities, or beyond what your customer/prospect could commit to at this call;

realistic – it must not be so easy that achieving it contributes nothing to the progress of the sale or your relationship with your customer/prospect;

timed – it must contain a time limit by which you will have fulfilled your objective.

Thus, 'Sell Mr Marks 600 widgets' does not express a **SMART** call objective; nor is 'Get a referral appointment to see Mrs Smith'. These 'statements of intent' could be better expressed **SMART**ly as:

> To persuade Mr Marks at this visit to take
> 600 widgets plus corresponding spares, and
> give our products a trial in demonstrations
> over a minimum 4 weeks.

> To convince Mr White at this call to refer
> me to Mrs Smith for a 30-minute interview
> today.

These objectives are *specific*, they clearly state *what* must be achieved, *when* they must be achieved, and both contain a *measurement* against which performance can be judged. If we assume that they are also achievable and realistic, such **SMART** objectives will tie you down to a precise goal and concentrate your energy on what you are at the call to achieve. **SMART** call objectives will discipline you and minimise unprofitable meandering from the task.

Unfortunately, it does happen that sometimes you make calls when factors you predicted *might* occur, but you hoped never would, actually do occur and prevent you achieving your call objective. Is there any way of minimising this problem of calls that divert sharply from expectations?

One option is to weigh up the new factors and revise your call objectives on the spot, and assume that the revised objective really is the best that you could have achieved in the circumstances. Some salespeople can do this, but others find that trying to think constructively and plan a new approach while actually with a buyer may be less than successful, and results in a revised objective that is more of an ego-saver than a genuinely useful business goal.

Another option is to consider potential objective-inhibiting factors during your pre-call planning, and prepare two types of call objective: a *primary* objective and a *secondary* (or fallback) objective.

A primary objective represents the maximum that is achievable at a call; the ideal. It is the goal that the interview must lead to. It will not necessarily be easy, but if achieved it will be a significant result.

A secondary objective is something less which, if secured, will still progress the sale and enable you to retrieve something of real value from your interview. A pre-planned secondary objective gives you a rational fallback position for when those unhoped-for factors do occur, and a sound basis from which to negotiate a revised offer, rather than allowing the pressure of the situation to compromise your clear thinking. The strength and confidence you can gain from a predetermined fallback position is immeasurable.

Recording objectives

To help you focus on your objectives in the often dynamic exchanges that take place during a sales interview, particularly when it is one in a series of long-term, high-value interviews, you may find it useful to record call objectives on a planning format.

At its simplest, a planning format looks like this:

Customer/Prospect _____

Contact name _____

Date of visit _____

PRIMARY CALL OBJECTIVES

SECONDARY (fallback) OBJECTIVES

For some, planning formats may need to be more comprehensive, and include space not only for primary and secondary call objectives, but also for notes on other aspects of the meeting.

The complexity of the detail you need to put on the planning format you use will depend on the kind of call you make and the nature of your business. In any event, the principal values of a planning format should be as follows.

● **Discipline** A planning format must be seen as a commitment. You resolve not to walk away from a call until you have secured, as a minimum, the secondary call objective (which you predetermined would still serve the purpose of your visit, even though it is not the maximum that you could have attained).

● **Focus**   If you keep your planning slip literally in your view (though not in your customer's/prospect's), or at least in mind, throughout an interview, you can be sure of never losing sight of what you are at the call to achieve. This may seem to be an obvious point to make; but perhaps there have been times when you have momentarily lost the control of an interview to your customer, or the customer has thrown irrelevant points into the conversation or it has been highly animated – and suddenly you wonder what you are supposed to be doing. A glance at the objectives on your planning slip will refocus your thoughts on to the task at hand, and allow you to keep the meeting on track.

● **Revision**   Of course there will be times when facts that materially affect your planning objectives only emerge during an interview. If the objectives are written out beforehand, it will be easier for you to revise them – and still maintain realism – than it will be to organise **SMART** objectives under your contact's gaze.

So to sum up: call objectives provide a target for the meeting. With a defined target to aim for, the interview can be steered towards an intended conclusion. And, knowing the end-point means that the sales opening can be planned with great precision.

Finally – do not forget yourself

At this point it is worth mentioning that you should not forget to plan the visible impact you will make on the meeting. Details are all too easy to neglect, and this may be compounded by haste. A conscious effort and decision to match appearance broadly to the prospect's expectations is well worth while.

This involves a number of factors, some practical (someone selling to farmers needs to keep wellington boots in the car), others more to do with image. There is a fine line between a smart suit and a sharp suit. A salesperson can to a degree reflect the prevailing standards of the customer, for example selling to advertising agencies whose employees are all fashionably dressed may mean doing likewise (though not, perhaps, out-doing them!). Common sense is the best guide, and, if in doubt, remain conventional and smart in a professional way. Describing the objective in terms of what competencies you wish to project, rather than simply what appearance you have may help find the right balance; if the prevailing impression needs to be of efficiency, expertise, or one of technical competence, then your appearance must be designed to establish just that. Some sales-people lose important elements of a good first impression because they look 'tatty'. Clearly, being smartly dressed, well turned out and with appropriate attention to detail (clean finger-nails and shoes, for instance) are important. Should you want to check this area in more detail, or seek specific advantage from aspects of appearance, a good reference is *Your Total Image: How to communicate success* by Philippa Davies (Piatkus).

It is equally important that you should project an appearance of efficiency; by which is meant a little more than simply being efficient. For example, your briefcase or sample case should be tidy and well organised. Your calculator should have batteries in, visual aids should be ready, accessible and in the right order. A moment's thought, such as keeping shoe polish in the car, can make small but important differences to appearances. And as Oscar Wilde said, 'It is only shallow people who do not judge by appearances.'

Overall, when a sales meeting turns out well, it rarely has anything much to do with chance (good luck is only useful to explain why your competitors are successful). It is more likely to be because it was well researched, well planned and set up; and subsequently well executed.

We will now turn to the opportunities that lie within the phrase 'well executed', the detail of the face-to-face encounter.

4

A Basis for Meeting – *the structure and manner*

No customer is worse than no customer.
Sign in department store

A sales meeting is a dynamic thing. It is a meeting involving two people with different thoughts, views and intentions, yet with potentially a common aim; to do business. To make the face-to-face meeting successful is, as we have already seen, dependent on many things, not least on the ability of the salesperson to chart a course through this unpredictable encounter, and to do so in a way that encourages the prospect to feel the process is useful and that he stands to gain from it.

We referred earlier to the structure of the sales and buying process. This must form the foundation of everything that happens face-to-face, and must be kept in mind as an element of the 'route map' you need to guide you through the meeting.

Start by considering how people buy; how they make a decision to purchase, or not. Classically their thinking moves through seven stages.

– I am important and I want to be respected.
– Consider my needs.
– How will your ideas help me?
– What are the facts?
– What are the snags'?
– What shall I do?
– I approve (or not).

This seems like common sense, indeed if you think about it, you will find it is what you do. A good analogy is that of 'weighing up' the case or argument, putting all the good points on one side, all the less good on the other and assessing the net effect.

Any attempt that responds unsatisfactorily to any of these stages is unlikely to end in agreement. The buyer's mind has to be satisfied on each point before moving to the next, and to be successful the persuading sequence must match this decision-making sequence, and run parallel to it.

Table 4.1 shows the process alongside the persuasive objectives, what you are trying to achieve at each stage and the technique employed in any communication. The two keys to success are the process of matching the other person's progression and describing, selectively, your case, and discussing it in a way that relates to the circumstances of the other person.

Table 4.1 Decision-making process

Decision sequence	Persuasion objectives	Persuasion stages
I am important Consider my needs	To create rapport, generate interest or acceptance. To find out about them and their needs	1. Opening
What are the facts?	To state a case that will be seen as balanced in favour of action	2. Stating the case
What are the snags?	Preventing or handling negative reactions that may unbalance the argument (objections)	3. Handling objections
What shall I do? I approve	Obtaining a commitment to action, or to a step in the right direction (purchase)	4. Injunction to act (close)

When persuasion works, both parties will have gone through this sequence stage by stage. However, if the attempt to persuade is unsuccessful, it will often be found that:

– the sequence has not taken place at all;
– some stage has been missed out;
– the sequence has been followed too quickly or too slowly, which means the salesperson is at one stage when the prospect wants to be, and expects the salesperson to be, at another. The two processes must proceed in tandem.

Early on, because people may well need to go through a number of stages – they may want proposals in writing, to confer with a colleague or run a test of the product being sold – you may not always be able to aim immediately for a commitment to buy. You must, however, have some other, clear objective on which to get a commitment. A positive 'yes' to your putting in a written proposal is a good step in the right direction. The persuasion of what you are doing throughout the process must be lined up towards such an end.

Imagine, as a simple example, that a secretary wants the boss to buy a new typewriter. The ultimate objective is for them to say 'Yes, buy it' about a particular machine. But it may be a step in the right direction to get them to review some brochures, check the quality of what the present machine produces, have a demonstration, get a quote and so on. Sometimes there are many steps to be gone through before the ultimate objective can be achieved. Progressing through each, like taking steps up a ladder, is significant in reaching the end point, whether it is the top of the ladder or the objective we have set. In selling interim objectives may include agreement to accept a trial, a sample or a demonstration; a request for a quotation or written proposal and so on.

Whatever your objective is, however, it is important to know and to be able to recognise the various stages ahead. With any individual contact you can identify the following.

● What stage has been reached in the decision process.
● Whether your sequence matches it.
● If not, why not?

- What do you need to do if the sequence does not match?
- Has a step been missed?
- Are you going too fast?
- Should you go back in the sequence?
- Can your objectives still be achieved, or were they the wrong objectives?
- How can you help the other person through the rest of the buying process?

Naturally, the whole process is not always covered in only one contact between salesperson and prospect; several meetings or exchanges may be necessary.

SALES EDGE 3 | Understand the Structure

- understand how the customer views the process
- use their thinking process to help you sell
- aim everything towards the close
- monitor and adapt as you proceed

The structure of the buying/selling process is the basis for all that follows. On the sales side, an understanding of how people make buying decisions is the foundation of sales success. You should aim firmly towards the close, but always bear the customer's view firmly in mind. This makes what you do at every stage more effective, and helps you to view every sales contact as a unique event.

Be conscious of what you are doing throughout the process

Making it acceptable

There are two factors that, together, make your manner acceptable. They should be an appropriate blend of 'projection' and of 'empathy'. What exactly do these terms mean? Well, by 'projection' we mean the way we come across to others, and particularly the confidence, credibility and 'clout' with which we come over; or at least appear to come over. By 'empathy' we mean simply the ability to put yourself in the other person's shoes and see things from their point of view. Not only to see them, but also to *be seen to do so*.

It is possible to categorise four distinct types of sales approach on an axis of high and low projection, and high and low empathy. This is illustrated in Figure 4.2.

Figure 4.2 The four types of sales approach

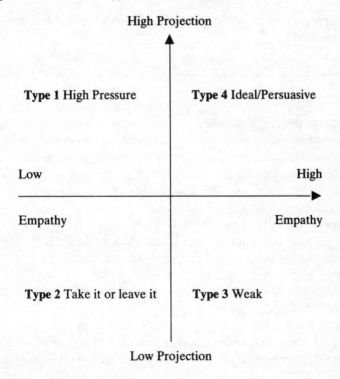

47

SALES EDGE 4 | **Adopt the Right Manner**

- be conscious of the manner you adopt
- tailor your approach to the customer
- make sure you appear professional
- always see, and respond, to the customer's views

If we are honest, salespeople are not involved in everyone's favourite profession. At worst the archetypal hard-sell, high-pressure sales approach switches people off. And so it should. Therefore, there is no room for an unprofessional approach. If the manner adopted adds throughout the process to the customer seeing you as the exception rather than the rule, as they might put it, as a professional – then it adds to your effectiveness.

Always use empathy, and project in a way that builds credibility

---

Type 1: the 'high-pressure' salesperson is over-aggressive and insensitive. *They* may feel they win the argument but, in fact, their projection, without empathy, becomes self-defeating and switches people off. The archetypal high-pressure person is the popular image of, say, the double-glazing salesperson.

Type 2: the 'take it or leave it' salesperson has little interest either in the other person, nor, curiously, his own ideas. A lack of commitment to the whole process tends to let it run into the sand. The archetypal take it or leave it person is the kind of unhelpful shop assistant with whom most of us are all too familiar.

Type 3: the 'weak' communicator is the sort of person of which it is said, disparagingly, 'they mean well'. And so they do, they have good sensitivity to the other person, and come over as essentially nice, but take the side of the listener so much on occasion that persuasion vanishes and they achieve nothing.

The Customer

Selling needs to focus on the customer; and all customers are different. First, there are the inherent differences between individuals. We cannot do much about that, except watch for it, react, adapt and avoid being censorious. It is important not to find yourself thinking, and perhaps allowing it to show, 'Why *on earth* does he think that?'. Everyone's priorities and perspectives are not the same. We must allow this, and work with it.

Secondly, it is possible to categorise customers, at least in a general sense and in a way that helps you to get off on the right foot with them, and run a better meeting thereafter. The sort of way this is usually represented is shown in Figure 4.3 on page 50, contrasting just two differing factors on two axes which reflect customers' attitudes and approaches to buying and salespeople.

This produces a list of four types, and they are sufficiently different to demand different approaches. This is perhaps best described with reference to their likely differing attitudes to salespeople, stated below, in quotes, as a customer might describe them.

Type 1: (assertive – cold)

'Salespeople cannot be trusted. They are determined to sell me something I neither want nor need. I must therefore be tough and resistant. The best defence against salespeople is offence.'

Type 2: (accommodating – cold)

'Salespeople cannot be trusted. To defend myself I try to avoid them. I stay as uninvolved as possible.'

Figure 4.3 Customers' attitudes

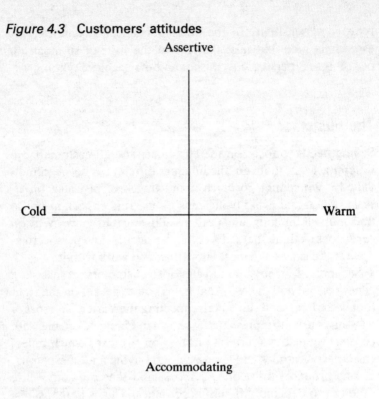

Type 3: (accommodating – warm)

'Many products I am responsible for buying are very much alike. Since it doesn't matter to me which one I buy, I prefer to buy from a salesperson I like and who likes me. I like to try to make friends with all the salespeople who call.'

Type 4: (assertive – warm)

'I buy things which it has been demonstrated will benefit me and my company. I buy from salespeople who prove they can help me, by offering products and a quality of service which exactly satisfies my needs.'

The usefulness of such a picture can be illustrated by looking at the best way of approaching the opening stage with each:

How to open a sale with type 1 (assertive) customers

- Do not expect a warm welcome.
- Accept their negative attitude, and use your professionalism as a foil.
- Keep small talk to an absolute minimum.
- Emphasise that you are there for sound business reasons.
- Make your opening remarks short and very much to the point.
- Do not be intimidated.
- Do not try to be clever by using what these people will consider salespeople's 'ploys'.
- Appear to let them take the lead, but demonstrate your *control* of the interview by attentive listening, note taking, and asking concise, factual and open questions, which will, in fact, help direct the meeting.
- Be firm and polite but never appear subservient.
- Position yourself as confident, professional and calmly determined.

How to open a sale with type 2 (accommodating/ cool) customers

- Expect these people to appear cool and distant, and understand that you will be seen as a threat to their security until you have won their trust.
- Be calm, professional and unhurried.
- Avoid pressure tactics.
- Do not say too much during the opening moments of an interview. Let them 'size you up' for themselves, and do not cloud their picture of you by being flashy, brash or pushy.
- Some small talk is recommended.
- Do not expect to make a sale on your first visit to these people.
- Position yourself as an adviser.

How to open a sale with type 3 (accommodating/ warm) customers

- Expect a warm welcome, but understand that these people welcome everyone: their warmth does not necessarily mean you are particularly special.
- Allow them to express their feelings with some small talk, but stay in control and do not let them lose sight of the fact that you are there for business reasons.
- As these people like to feel they belong to select groups, mention as early as possible the involvement your company has had with other comparable, reputable companies.
- Tell them exactly how you would like to structure the interview, including your role and theirs.
- Do not appear too officious or clinical by producing brochures or samples too early, or by taking too many notes: keep the opening conversational.
- Position yourself as a friendly purchase recommender.

How to open a sale with type 4 (assertive) customers

- Expect a correct and professional greeting with a firm handshake.
- Take your seat unhurriedly and prepare openly for the interview by taking out of your briefcase the documentation – including a notepad – which you will need.
- Demonstrate your own professionalism, and understand that these people will expect your acknowledgement of their commercial skills.
- Your opening remarks must be natural (not contrived), short and clearly indicate that you already know a fair amount about their company.
- Do not be dogmatic: they will want you to be flexible so that their ideas and objectives can be accommodated in a *joint* solution.
- Be prepared to revise your call objectives.

- Avoid a fixed or rigid 'standard interview' approach.
- Position yourself as a creative, experienced problem solver.

Respect for the customer's individuality, taking an accurate view of what 'type' of customer you are dealing with and making a real attempt to 'get on their wavelength' early on in the proceedings will always help you in any meeting. Sales technique is not, after all, something to be applied slavishly or by rote, but something to be deployed intelligently case by case. And the variable that dictates exactly how that deployment should vary is the customer. Every customer is different, and it is a dangerous mistake to treat them as if they were all alike.

Remember also that, at the prospect's office, you are on their territory. You should respect it. It sounds obvious enough, but do not sit down until asked; do not even ask to smoke unless it is clear (perhaps because an ashtray is on the desk) that this is not likely to offend; do not bang your hard briefcase on his polished desk; and do not get too close, people do not like being crowded – so respect their space.

Be considerate of anything and everything that will indicate a caring manner, one that respects the customer, their views and their property. They will appreciate the attitude this displays.

Now let us turn, in Chapter 5, to the way we progress through a meeting, to see how the attitudes described here are used stage by stage as the meeting progresses.

5

Face-to-Face – *making it persuasive*

> The meek shall inherit the earth, but they
> will never increase market share.
> *William McGowan*

In Chapter 4 we looked at the decision-making process used by the customer to make buying decisions. We will now relate the seven stages involved to the four main stages of the face-to-face meeting; that is opening, presenting the case, handling objections and closing. This is the real route map, what has to be borne in mind here is not a fixed way forward, but a structure and approach which will guide the way through the conversation, enabling the salesperson to maintain the initiative and yet make what is going on entirely acceptable to the prospect.

The route map analogy is a good one. You have to keep the full picture in front of you and, even if selecting different choices along the route, keep moving in the right direction. In addition, the fine detail is important; miss one signpost and you are off the route and will perhaps be lost. Similarly, the detail is important here, as we move through the four stages. Small – perhaps seemingly basic – details are as important to the success of the whole encounter as the big issues.

The first stage is, of course, the opening. This is, as we shall see, a little more than just a series of introductory exchanges; it sets the scene for the whole meeting.

1. Opening the Sale

It is a funny thing about meetings; you may have noticed that they have two beginnings. One is ritual. It is concerned with the initial remarks such as 'Good morning', but also 'Did you find our offices OK?', 'What a dreadful day, nothing but rain the whole summer' (so what else is new?). Remarks like this allow us to get into the swing of things. Then, someone, often the buyer, says something like, 'Right, what I suggest we do this morning is . . .', and the meeting starts again. You know the feeling.

This area is worthy of consideration, but with care we are, after all, only talking about a minute or two and must not get ridiculously psychological about it (certainly it takes longer to review than actually to happen). But it is important. We want to run and direct the meeting. Not in an unpleasant sense from the point of view of the customer; the trick is *to run the kind of meeting you want, and the customer finds he likes* (and preferably likes more than any meetings he has with your competitors). Only one person can effectively be 'in charge'. There is a line in Shakespeare's *Much Ado about Nothing* that says when 'Two men ride off on a horse, one must ride behind'. This certainly makes the point. If the salesperson does not get hold of the meeting the customer surely will. So, what can we do about this?

The answer lies in those first, ritual moments. Unless the initiative is taken then, it may not be possible to take it for some time; at worst it will be completely lost. Specifically, this means keeping the conversation off the weather or whatever, and contributing something more businesslike which still fulfils the ritual process. The two tactics outlined below make good examples.

Appeal to pride

When using this tactic you comment on something positive about the customer's business. This could be simply an observation of how smart their new reception area looks, 'I'm sure it impresses all your customers', or may come from your research, 'I noticed in last week's trade papers how successful you have been with the export initiative in the Far East'. Good research will mean you know your customer will be able to say, 'Yes, I'm very pleased about that'. This kind of comment shows an interest, it shows you have done some checking and it provides a ritual moment of *relevant* conversation.

Good turns

This approach is very effective with people you see regularly.

A good exponent of the 'good turn' approach is a salesman who comes to see me regularly. He notes the kind of work I do, the kind of industries I work in and will often arrive with, say, a magazine article in his briefcase. 'I know you do a lot in the hotel and travel industry,' he might say, 'I wondered if you had seen this?' Seen it or not, I like the approach and it often produces something interesting. It costs him, of course, nothing except a little time and attention.

Many similar actions can be taken and then the salesperson can move on to say 'Let's get down to business', from which control of the meeting follows more naturally.

SALES EDGE 5 | Direction

- take the initiative
- lead the meeting
- make the customer feel this is natural and right

Getting hold of the meeting, being in charge, makes an excellent start to the proceedings. Run the kind of meeting *you* want, and which they find they like – and preferably like better than anything being done by your competitors.

Start off in charge; stay in charge

At the same time the beginning of the opening should flow through a structure, if only to avoid starting with the trite phrases of the less professional salesperson: 'I just happened to be passing'; 'How's business?' and so on.

The elements to be orchestrated at the beginning are:

A greeting + **an interest-** + **the reason for calling**
creating
comment

plus

either **a check for any** *or* **the first fact-finding**
outstanding **question**
issues

The greeting

Obviously, your greeting must be right for the time of day! But also for the depth of your relationship and your customer's/ prospect's personality type. This means that even long-standing customers can still expect a formal greeting, whereas some prospects respond well to an informal greeting. In any doubt, take the formal route.

The question of whether and when to use first names can only be answered within the context of what your company recommends and what each contact finds acceptable. First-name use is more common now, but if in doubt remain more, rather than less, formal.

To make it just a little more likely that you will be remembered (after all the prospect may see many different salespeople), when it comes to introducing yourself it is best to use both your names – John Smith – and, at the same time, hand over a business card if you are meeting for the first time. (This is very much a ritual in other parts of the world; the Japanese even have waterproof plastic cards to use by the hotel pool!)

The interest-creating comment

There are two reasons for including in your opening words an interest-creating comment:

- to demonstrate your knowledge of and interest in your customer's/prospect's industry, company, people, plans, policies etc.;
- to begin the process of raising the contact's interest in and level of receptivity to you and what you are there for.

The reason for calling

This must be expressed as a buyer benefit. If a relationship already exists between you and a customer you should be easily able to devise a highly relevant benefit; if there is no relationship, you must choose a benefit which experience tells you that most customers have found valuable. For instance, with a regular customer the objective may be linked to selling the range, introducing products the customer has not, as yet, tried. If the product shows, let us say, a cost saving in his production, then the benefit is the greater cost benefits of extending his use of the product range. The customer is not likely to be interested in buying more of the range simply because he likes you. This kind of thinking needs to come over, whichever customer is being approached.

A check for outstanding issues

In some industries, for example book publishing or healthcare, it is common practice for a supplier to take back unsold products.

It may well be the best approach to encourage a customer to raise this, or other such outstanding matters, before you begin your current presentation, particularly when returns can be expected. This helps 'clear the decks'. If your customer's priority need is to resolve a problem concerning, say, current stock, this will be in the forefront of his or her mind. Until this need is satisfied he or she will not be receptive to the idea of buying new stock.

In such a case, helping your customer at the outset of an interview may give you some sort of minor bargaining chip; their initial view of you is then more positive.

The first fact-finding question

This is the bridge which links the interview opening with the interview proper. Your question should relate to the interest-creating comment and your reason for calling.

The following examples illustrate the four parts of an opening in action.

Example 1

Greeting	'Hello John. Good to see you again.'
Interest-creating comment	'I see that your company are moving into the DIY field as well.'
Reason for calling	'I'm sure we can help you stay ahead . . . even attract *new* customers . . . by brightening up the presentation of your displays – especially in the cut wood and garden paving areas.'
First fact-finding question	'Have you seen our new range of outdoor racking?'

Example 2

Greeting	'Good afternoon Dr Smith. John Brown from XYZ Healthcare. Thank you for seeing me. Your receptionist said you've had a busy surgery, so I'll be brief.'

Interest-creating comment	'As you know, this is the time of year when patients presenting with seasonal allergies can significantly increase the workload on health centres.'
Reason for calling	'We're introducing a new care pack which we believe will help ease the burden on GPs and nursing staff, and make patient management simpler and less expensive.'
First fact-finding question	'Could I begin by asking you about the number of patients presenting with [diseases] that you've seen this week?'

Example 3

Greeting	'Good morning Mr Jones. I hope you had a good holiday. You certainly seem to have found the sun.'
Interest-creating comment	'I know you've had tremendous success with your new children's section; in fact, your assistant said you were already thinking of expanding your range of teenage titles.'
Reason for calling	'It's the classics that are enjoying renewed popularity, as you know; and we're launching a new imprint starting with seven of the all-time best. They could create what you're looking for: a focal point to attract more children's sales.'

A check for outstanding issues	'Before we take a closer look at our lead titles, do you have any returns you'd like me to handle for you?'

Example 4

Greeting	'Hello there, James; how are you?'
Interest-creating comment	'I have got together the details about service arrangements you asked for when I was here last week.'
Reason for calling	'It should only take 15/20 minutes to go through them together and see how they will work with your production schedule.'
First fact-finding question	'Did you get out the schedules we discussed?'

Of course, this is not a set routine. There may be a more dramatic way of creating an impact and getting a hearing. I once met a particular airline representative. One of his jobs was to call on travel agents and brief many members of their staff, updating them on schedules, fares etc. Traditionally this was done by moving round the office talking to each in turn. It worked, but was time-consuming. With certain bigger accounts he had another approach.

He arrived, from a nearby sandwich shop, with a tray of coffee and doughnuts. He was able to gather the majority of the staff around him for a coffee break, and later pick up individually the odd ones left manning the phones. It worked well, and the 'doughnut-man' achieved good co-operation from his major accounts. Every business needs thinking about in terms of how such individual, and distinctive, impact can be made.

This idea will not, of course, be right for everyone. It does, however, demonstrate the right kind of thinking, such an approach may prompt other ideas. Other approaches are more generally applicable. Suggesting, for example, an agenda can help you get hold of the meeting. An agenda that suits you, but also makes sense to the customer, and is phrased carefully: 'It might be most helpful to you, Mr Customer, if we were to take . . . first, then . . .'. This is a good example of sales technique coming over to the customer as helpful and focusing on his needs. He is at liberty to amend your suggestion, but you are both likely to end up following broadly your suggestion.

Having made a good start, there is still a great deal going on in the opening stages of the sale. Perhaps the most important is concerned with finding out about customers, and their needs.

Identification of customer needs

Customer attitudes vary at the beginning of interviews. They can be friendly, hostile, indifferent, interested, helpful or defensive. The opening of an interview is a crucial time for both parties.

Remember the first two steps in the systematic way people approach any buying decision outlined in the previous chapter:

- I am important and want to be respected;
- consider my needs.

These two steps make the salesperson's objectives at the beginning of an interview very clear:

- to make a customer feel important in the salesperson's eyes (to which the preliminaries contribute); and
- to agree to the customer's stated needs.

Successful selling is particularly dependent on this stage in the process being well handled. Exploring and identifying the customer's needs correctly makes them want to hear your proposition. Subsequently, making it attractive reduces the possibility of objections and thus obtains more voluntary commitment.

Remember, people act to relieve a felt need. Where the need is low, the solution has a high impact, either positively or negatively, depending on the way it is offered. Sometimes customers will volunteer their needs clearly. More often, needs have to be explored, identified and spelt out before we can move on.

SALES EDGE 6 | Identifying Needs

- ask the right questions, in the right way
- be more precise and thorough than your competitors in finding out what the customers really want
- find out their real reasons for these needs

It is not putting it too strongly to suggest that this is a 'sheep and goats' factor in selling. That is, those who find out more about client needs, and are seen to do so by the client, have a head start on everything else that follows.

Get a firm basis of information; it can be the first step to beating competition

---

Exploration can be carried out by either questions or statements, or by a combination of both questions and statements. Questions are initially safer and more productive, but they have to be carefully and correctly used. The precise method of questioning technique most likely to bring results utilises four basic types of question, which are used in sequence to probe for more information – and information of a less general nature that is more focused on what the customer really wants and why. The four types of question you can use are as follows.

Background questions
For example, 'What's your unit cost per item?'

Problem questions
For example, 'Are unit costs a problem?'

Implication questions
For example, 'What effect are high unit costs having on the rest of the business?'

Need questions
For example, 'What would you like to happen as far as unit costs are concerned?'

Open or closed questions can be equally successful, but open questions (ones that cannot be answered with a 'yes' or 'no') encourage the client to talk and produce more information.

The type and combination of questions used is very important. Experience shows that asking fewer background questions but focusing them better, asking more problem questions, amplifying problems by asking implication questions, and converting problems and implications into need questions works best, and forms a logical sequence. On the other hand asking a relatively large number of background questions, fewer problem, implication or need questions, and introducing solutions after the stage of asking background questions works less well.

The reason for this difference is simple. The first sequence follows the customer's buying sequence, while the latter makes salespeople talk about themselves, their firms and their products/ services, which distances the approach from the customer.

Each type of question also has an equivalent approach based on a statement for which the same sequence can be used. This is background – problems – implications – needs, and statements can be most confidently used when there is already a thorough understanding of the customer's situation. Thus, they are more often used after questioning or during subsequent meetings.

Customers with strongly felt needs will often buy with very little encouragement. Many, however, are satisfied with existing solutions. Faced with this situation then we must, in fact, create some dissatisfaction before the customer will consider a change. (This is explored in more detail when we look at *Creating (or extending) needs*, see page 67.).

A final point about questioning. You do not just have to ask questions, you have to *listen* to the answers; and what you do next should be based on those answers. If you proceed apparently as if you had not heard, and the prospect feels they are hearing the 'standard pitch', something that bears no relation to their spoken requirements, you will naturally not be so well received.

SALES EDGE 7 | **Listening**

- listen very carefully
- concentrate on listening
- take note of what is said
- be *seen* to be a good listener
- adapt what you plan to do in light of what you hear

This is very simple (at least to state). Good salespeople are good listeners. It is said that mankind was created with two ears and one mouth and that should be a reflection on their use. It is very easy to find that we are not listening – really listening – to customers. Below you will find some hints for making sure your listening is effective.

Listen actively and note the information you obtain

Active listening to obtain information

1. **WANT TO LISTEN** This is easy once you realise how useful it is to the sales process.

2. **LOOK LIKE A GOOD LISTENER** If they can see they have your attention, customers will be more forthcoming.

3. **UNDERSTAND** It is not just the words but what lies behind them that you must note.

4. **REACT** Let them see you have heard, understood and are interested. Nods, small comments etc. will encourage.

5. **STOP TALKING** Other than small comments, you cannot listen and talk simultaneously. Do not interrupt

6. **USE EMPATHY** Put yourself in the other person's shoes and make sure you really appreciate their point of view.

7. **CHECK** If necessary, ask questions to clarify matters as the conversation proceeds. An understanding based, even partly, on guesses is dangerous. But ask diplomatically, do not say 'You did not explain that very well'.

8. **REMAIN UNEMOTIONAL** Too much thinking ahead ('However will I cope with that objection?') can distract.

9. **CONCENTRATE** Allow nothing to distract you.

10. **LOOK AT YOUR CUSTOMER** Nothing is read more rapidly as disinterest than an inadequate focus of attention.

11. **NOTE PARTICULARLY THE KEY POINTS** Edit what you are told to make what you need to retain manageable.

12. **AVOID PERSONALITIES** It is the ideas and information that matters, not what you think of the person; this can distract.

13. **DO NOT LOSE YOURSELF IN SUBSEQUENT ARGUMENT** Some thinking ahead may be necessary (you listen faster than they talk, so it is possible); too much and you suddenly find you have missed something.

14. **AVOID NEGATIVES** To begin with at least, signs of disagreement (even visually) can make the customer clam up.

15. **MAKE NOTES** Do not trust your memory, and if it is polite to do so, ask permission.

Agreeing needs

Discovering customer needs, while it may be an important step, is not all that needs to be done. While knowing what the customer wants, and why he wants it, will help; if the information is obtained in a way which makes it clear to the customer exactly what you know – this will do more. The customer must know you know, and this is important; it implies *agreement* of needs. What does this mean in practice? Well, that you do not just say to yourself, as perhaps a print salesman might, 'so he is interested in quality work'. Nor is it sufficient if you discover why, 'because promotional print has an impact on his customers'. On such key issues this has to be checked back. The customer must be *asked*, 'It is not just quality work you are after in an academic sense, it is something that will guarantee the right impact on your customers, is that right?'. If the answer is affirmative you know you are on target. It may also be more useful later to refer back to this in a way that recaps, '*You* did say impact on customers was the important thing', rather than suggest, 'It seems to *me* therefore that what you want is . . .'.

So, can you now move on to presenting your case, sure that everyone's needs are understood and agreed? Sorry, no; there is still more to be done before the opening stage is complete.

Creating (or extending) needs

As the conversation progresses, there may be an opportunity to *create* needs. Sometimes this is done by helping customers discover needs of which they were unaware. More often it can involve suggesting that marginal differences in need are better met by your product or service than by that of someone else. In this case it may be necessary to create dissatisfaction with an existing supplier. And this must be done carefully. If not, it will be seen as critical of the customer's previous buying decisions, this will be resented and, at worst, may lead to an argument. Rather, the salesperson will have to show that the situation is unsatisfactory due to factors outside the customer's control by mentioning, for example, such factors as:

- other suppliers' poor delivery record;
- other suppliers' bad service;
- poor design standards.

In addition, questioning will often identify hidden, unstated needs, sometimes beyond an initially stated position.

With that in mind, there is still one more thing involved in the opening stage.

Establishing priorities

Customers often have a mix of needs. This is not surprising, especially when technical or complex products or services are being bought. As questioning reveals the needs it may well be that conflicts become apparent, 'I want this delivered immediately, tailored to our requirements and at the lowest possible quote'. All these factors may be possible, individually. But which is most important?

Early delivery may be possible with items from a standard range, and this may meet the need reasonably well. But will it be well enough? If the buyer really wants a tailored solution, is he prepared to wait for delivery? And so on and so on. There may be a neat list of three key priorities, or a complex picture of many different factors to be taken into account. In either case the principle is the same, we have to try to sort out the customer's priorities, not simply form a view of what the priorities would be for most customers (much less what *we* think they should be). Again, this adds to our information base and can be of great use as the meeting progresses, guiding us towards the right presentation, one that reflects the customer's priorities.

So far so good

At the end of the opening stage what sort of view should the customer have of the salesperson? Assume that they have never met before. The initial impressions are important. The immediate view should be of someone professional; that is well turned out, getting down to business positively, having an instant customer orientation, likely to know what they are talking about, well organised and, overall, worth giving a hearing.

The opening stage should build on this first view. As it progresses, then to the above should be added a feeling that the way the salesperson is working is tailored to the customer, in other words what is being said is 100 per cent appropriate; evidence that they are appreciating, understanding and getting to grips with the customer's point of view; and perhaps, as appropriate to the kind of business involved, they are:

– technically competent;
– numerate;
– avoiding inappropriate jargon;
– creative;
– prepared to listen;

and, very important, the customer must feel they are interested in him, and, ideally, interesting to deal with.

2. Presenting the Case

This second stage of the face-to-face meeting is the core of the whole sales process.

Once needs are identified and priorities established, the next step is to show how satisfaction will come from the specific products/services or recommendations that are offered. Again the action springs from the appropriate stage of the buying process. If we remember the seven-points involved in a decision to buy, the customer's mental demands are now:

– will your ideas help me?
– what are the snags?

This means that the salesperson has four objectives as he presents his case: to make his ideas understandable, attractive and convincing (this is what we mean by *persuasive*), and to get feedback that the first three objectives have been achieved.

Each of these elements must be considered in turn and then deployed together in a cohesive and effective conversation.

Making ideas understandable

This is the basis of all communication, and is especially important in *persuasive* communication. Now, of all the things you do in selling, the core process of telling people about your product or service is the one you no doubt feel you do best. Whatever else, people understand you. Or do they? Communication is never as straightforward as it might seem. Misunderstandings occur all too easily and clarity must be achieved before persuasion is possible. Achieving clarity should not be taken for granted; a mistake which can easily be made as you relate something you know well and deal with regularly.

Without taking due care, however, you may find someone saying 'What do you mean?' in response to something you have said. Sometimes you initiate the correction, 'But I meant . . .' and sometimes too people will say to you 'You want me to do *what*?'. Because, as has been said, communication is not always as easy as it seems; and this shows itself in a number of ways.

It can suffer from being unclear, '. . . you fit the thingy on to that sprocket thing and . . .' (just try it). Or imprecise, '. . . then it's about a mile' (three miles later . . .). It can be so full of jargon that we find ourselves saying manual excavation device, instead of spade. Or it can be gobbledegook, 'Considerable difficulty has been encountered in the selection of optimum materials and experimental methods, but this problem is being attacked vigorously and we expect the development phase will proceed at a satisfactory rate.' (We are looking at the handbook and trying to decide what to do.) So much so that the sense is diluted. There are innumerable barriers to communication, not least the assumptions, prejudices and inattention of those on the receiving end.

All this may simply cause a bit of confusion, and take a moment to sort out, or it can cause major problems either immediately or later. But there is never more likely to be problems than when there is an intention to get someone to *do* something, i.e. to buy from you. At least as many sales are probably lost simply because the customer is not clear about what, exactly what, the salesperson means, as are ever lost for any other reasons. It is an area that is worth giving some thought and consideration. What helps to make communication clear? Three factors are key, they are as follows.

Structure and sequence

Presentations should always be structured around the customer's needs. Here is an example. 'So in choosing a system, your first concern is compatibility, your second is simplicity, and your third is productivity. Let's look at the compatibility aspect first, and then deal with the others . . .' You cannot, frankly, label things in advance too often. Such an approach keeps the flow of the argument clear and organised. It is also important to conclude one aspect before moving to the next, and to take matters in a logical order.

Visual aids

People understand and remember more when information is presented in visual form. Charts, diagrams, slides, pictures and brochures can all strengthen the clarity of the presentation. In using them follow the basic rules, keep them hidden until they are needed, keep quiet while they are being examined (people cannot concentrate properly on two things at once) and remove them after use to avoid any distraction. Customers like it too if some of the material has clearly been produced specially for your meeting with them.

Jargon

Every company and industry, particularly if its products are technical, has its own language or jargon. Some jargon can be useful, if pitched at the right level, but overall the presentation must use the customer's language. This means using words and terms you are certain the customer understands, and avoiding words or terms which can be misinterpreted in any way, e.g. 'our product is cheap', 'we have a fragmented range of services . . .'.

In a technical business, the aspect of making things understood, clearly understood, can be easily overlooked (you may feel you need some help in making things more persuasive, but surely not simply in explaining the firm, its services or a particular approach). Make sure you really do explain clearly. Many prospects are lost solely because they are confused.

SALES EDGE 8 | **Clarity**

- make what you say immediately understandable
- make explanations thorough and precise
- beware of jargon

If the customer cannot understand you there is no way you will be found persuasive. Never underestimate the difficulty of clear communication, even on topics you know well, and remember that anything technical will compound the problem. Get this right and, at best, you will be seen to be a ray of light among those who are less easy to follow. In every contact it will give you a clear run at all the other things you are trying to do.

Think about how to make things clear; clarity will create a foundation for persuasiveness

---

Making ideas attractive

People buy things for what they will do for them, or mean to them. It is the desirable results from the buyer's point of view (benefits) that are important, not what things are (features).

Often products or services can do many different things for customers, and not all customers want the same things done. Thus, only those benefits which meet the listener's needs should be mentioned, and it is the process of selecting and matching items from the total list of benefits to an individual customer's specific requirements that makes a particular idea, or solution, appear attractive.

There are normally three types of benefit which can be used; benefits to the listener in his job, or as a person, or benefits to others in which he is interested. The choice will depend on the listener's needs and priorities, though they are not mutually exclusive, as something may affect all three to a similar degree.

This benefit-oriented basis of description in talking with customers is vital. It is another 'sheep and goats' factor. The most successful salespeople do not sell products and services – they sell benefits; that is what customers want to buy. But what, exactly, are benefits? This is worth a moment's careful consideration.

Benefits are what products or services do for the customer. What they are is not important but what they do or mean for the customer is. To take an everyday example, a person does not buy an electric drill because he wants an electric drill, but because he wants to be able to make holes. He buys holes, not a drill. He buys the drill for what it will do (make holes) and this in turn may only be important to him because of a need for storage and a request to put up shelving.

Realising this not only makes selling more effective but also easier. You do not have to describe the same thing in the same way to a lot of different people, but meet each person's needs with potential benefits.

Benefits are what the product or service you sell can do for each individual customer – the things he wants them to do for him. Different customers buy the same thing for different reasons. It is important, therefore, to identify and use the particular benefits of interest to each. What a product 'does' is described by its benefits.

If this is forgotten, then the things which are important to a customer will not always be seen to be important from the salesperson's viewpoint. The result can, understandably, be a conflict of priorities with the customer focusing on one thing, while the salesperson focuses on the opposite, thus:

Customer	Salesperson
1. **Himself** Satisfaction of his needs	1. **Himself** His firm His product/service His ideas
2. **His needs and the benefits which satisfy them**	2. **His product/service and making the customer buy it**

3. **This salesperson** His firm His product/service His ideas	3. **Benefits to this customer**
4. **Buying from this salesperson**	4. **Customer's needs** Benefits which satisfy this customer's needs

This can be compounded if the sales persons' induction training has been introspective and presented predominantly from a technical or production viewpoint. Or, if training has not occurred at all.

The customer is most unlikely to see things from the salesperson's point of view. Each person is, to himself, the most important person in the world. Therefore, to be successful, the salesperson has to be able to see things from the customer's point of view, and demonstrate through his words and actions that he has done so. His chances of success are greater if he can understand the needs of the people he talks to and make them realise that he can fulfil those needs.

This is achieved essentially by the correct use of benefits. In presenting any proposition to a customer, even simply recommending something in reply to a query, you should always translate what you are offering into what it will do.

Often a firm grows introspective and product oriented (this is then all too often reflected in their product literature) and development can reinforce this attitude by adding more and more features. It is only a small step before everyone is busy trying to sell on features alone.

When competitors are almost identical in their performance – at least from a prospect's viewpoint, it can be difficult to sell benefits, since all suppliers seem to offer the same benefits. Choice then often depends on the personal appeal of the benefits in those features, rather than on the features themselves. Features are only important if they support the benefits the customer is interested in.

Deciding to concentrate on describing benefits is only half the battle, however. They have to be the right benefits. In fact, benefits are only important to a customer if they describe the satisfaction of his needs. Working out his needs, and then his benefits, means being 'in your customer's shoes'.

There are three types of benefit you can mention:

- benefits to the customer *in his job*, e.g. 'Order processing errors will be eliminated';
- benefits to your customer *as a person*, e.g. 'It will stop people complaining to you about order processing errors';
- benefits to *others in whom he is interested*, among colleagues, family, friends, etc., e.g. 'Customers will get the goods that they order'.

Which benefits are the most important? Again, the answer is those that fit in best with your customer's strategic and emotional needs, though they are not, of course, mutually exclusive.

When you think about your proposals you will be able to identify many benefits that can be derived from them; but beware of using too many, believing that the more you use, the more attractive your proposals become. The old saying, 'It's too good to be true' applies here. Too many benefits begin to stretch your customer's credulity.

You can, however, make your benefits more effective by *combining them in a logical sequence* so that, finally, your customer's need is met, e.g. 'With this computerised shelf allocation system, the best assortment of products is fitted into the space available [benefit]. This means that you get continuous sales of the high-volume lines [benefit] while making good margins on the slower movers [benefit]. Generally you optimise sales and profits from the available space, whatever it may be [benefit and need satisfaction]!'

To know what benefits to put forward, you must understand the needs of the buyer to whom you sell and the organisation he represents. Firms often have more than one decision-maker, so it is essential to pinpoint your contact within the hierarchy in order to relate to them accurately. See page 76.

Typical roles within the decision-making process

Users of service:
- may initiate;
- may specify;
- may veto.

Influencers:
- may help specify;
- may provide 'expert' objective opinion and information;
- may be outsiders;
- may be involved in setting criteria for judging between alternative suppliers.

Buyers:
- the unit that has formal authority to buy, or has an important influencing role on the decision to buy;
- may be measured on the primarily financial aspects (e.g. prices, discounts).

Deciders:
- may be the buyers;
- may be the end-users;
- are frequently the senior members of the end-user department;
- may well be the people who control the budget for the service.

Gatekeepers:
- those who control the flow of information (or lack of it) to others;
- may have the role of an influencer, a buyer or a decider.

To be sure of maximising the strength 'talking benefits' gives to what you say, it is useful to analyse products/services in terms of features and benefits, as follows.

Benefit	Feature
Has the ability to dispense tea and coffee simultaneously	Twin, 10-pint, heated containers (equipment for the catering trade)
Gives a better miles per gallon	Five-speed gearbox (motor car)
Easier and more comfortable (and perhaps therefore more productive) to use	Economic controls (machine tool)
Provides a quicker more certain analysis with less disruption of the accounts department	Computer-assisted audit (accountant)

Such an analysis (and it is a useful exercise to work this out point by point) will help differentiate between features and benefits. It is a useful ploy to present the benefits first; because where features lead, i.e. 'we can offer a computer-assisted audit', the customer response (mentally if not spoken) can too often be 'so what?'.

An analysis can be produced for any product or service, or for a range, and can be presented within a company to help everyone learn just what is a feature and what is a benefit.

The product feature/benefit analysis, shown in Table 5.1, sets out how this principle can be developed, showing a more detailed analysis of a particular product relating needs, benefits and features. As you look at this, note that the product analysis should be completed from left to right. Only when the needs have been identified can the appropriate benefits and relevant features be selected.

If the salesperson works from right to left, not only will he lose his buyer's interest as he talks about items which may not be of interest, but also he will have no basis for selecting benefits to stress.

Finally, remember that your 'customer' may in fact be a group of people, say the marketing, production and finance directors.

Each will have his own needs pattern, and therefore you must present benefits which occur with, in this case, three significantly different points of view. If this is done you produce a checklist, a prompt to conversation which will help lead you into the right kind of *descriptive* presentation.

Table 5.1   Features – Benefits – Needs Analysis

Agricultural Tractor

Customer needs	Benefits that will satisfy customer needs	Product features from which the benefits are derived
1. *Rational Performance* – must be able to work fast with a variety of implements	Plenty of power, particularly at low speeds	A 65 BHP diesel engine with high torque at low rpm. Wide range of matched implements available
Versatility – must cope with a variety of soil and cultivating conditions	Can travel at a wide variety of speeds	A 10-speed synchromesh gearbox – four wheel drive available for difficult conditions
Simplicity – must be easy to operate	Simple and speedy implement changeover. Easy to drive	Quick-attach linkage with snap-on hydraulic couplings. Ergonomically placed levers and pedals
Low cost – must be economical to run	Low fuel consumption	Efficient engine design with improved braking and fuel injector system. Good power/weight ratio

Reliability – must be able to operate continuously and be serviced quickly	Well-proven design with all basic snags removed. Local dealer with 24-hour parts service	More than 10,000 units already in operation. Wide dealer network with factory-trained mechanics backed by computerised parts operation
2. *Emotional Security* – (fear of making wrong decision)	Most popular tractor on the market – 10,000 farmers can't be wrong	Largest company in the industry with good reputation for reliability and value for money
Prestige – (desire to gain status in the eyes of others)	Chosen by those engaged in best agricultural practice	Favoured by agricultural colleges and large farmers

Reproduced from *20 Activities for Developing Sales Effectiveness*, Patrick Forsyth and Marek Gitlin (Gower, Aldershot, 1988).

The power of description can then be extended by relating benefits, different benefits, to the different people involved in the decision. For example, the rugged design of a computerised order processing system might mean:

Increased operator output and reduced fatigue	a benefit . . . to the supervisor
Improved levels of customer service, better company image and more repeat buying	a benefit . . . to the sales office manager
Saves cost, on maintenance and replacement	a benefit . . . to the financial manager

Such a format can be designed and used for each product/service, and any number of people across the decision-making process.

Note that not all the needs will be objective ones; most buyers also have subjective requirements bound up in their decisions. Even with technical things the final decisions can sometimes be heavily influenced by subjective factors, perhaps seemingly of minor significance, once all the objective needs have been met.

By matching benefits to individual customer's needs, you are more likely to make a sale, for the benefits must match a buyer's needs. The features only give rise to the right benefits.

Involvement and demonstration

It has long been said of selling motor cars, that the most important step is for the salesperson to get the prospect to sit in the driving seat. It is a manifestation of that Americanism 'ownership', but the lesson is clear; get the prospect to imagine the product or service in use and you will certainly be that much nearer to a sale.

This points back to what we have already mentioned about being descriptive (an element of 'talking benefits'), but also involves physical involvement. A couple of examples perhaps illustrate the point. Take a demonstration first. If a piece of equipment is being demonstrated, say, a word processing typewriter, then clearly the salesperson has to be able to demonstrate it effectively. They do not have to type fast, but they do have to be able to set up the machine, be familiar with the controls, be able to answer questions and so on. Further, they should be able to explain clearly and know how to get the prospect sitting at the keyboard experiencing the machine's excellence for him or herself. This means being able to guide them, and setting things up individually either for the experienced typist or the person with limited keyboard skills. All this applies even more if what is being demonstrated is more technical, complex or difficult to handle.

Demonstrations have to go right. If the prospect is left saying to themselves, 'Even the salesperson finds it difficult', they are hardly likely to buy.

A second example comes from the meetings industry. A conference organiser is looking round a hotel. He stands just inside the door of the room suggested for his planned event. The room is empty (or, sometimes, contains the last, messy, remnants of what went on there the previous day), and the salesperson points out the features. He lists the individually controllable lights, the good acoustics, the easy way in which equipment can be brought in and set up and so on. Alternatively, the conference buyer is taken right into the room. He is not told about the acoustics, they are demonstrated as the salesperson speaks to him from the far end of the room, he is offered the opportunity to try out his slides, he is taken to stand on the verandah where the morning break can be taken. Such an experience lets the person 'live' *their* event, imagine it happening – successfully – in that hotel, that room. It is not, or should not be, the standard tour, but is tailored to the person instead. An organising secretary will be made especially familiar with the reception area, and aspects of the meeting with which they will be involved.

A conference speaker will be encouraged to see how they feel on the platform. If the room can be laid out, even in part, as it will be on the day, so much the better.

In this way the prospect literally begins to take part in the selling process, and can leave the demonstration able to say 'I *know* it will work'. The prospects themselves can be another 'edge'.

SALES EDGE 9 | Talking Benefits

- understand the difference between features and benefits
- select the benefits appropriate to each customer
- lead with benefits

Talking benefits is always a basic component of an effective sales approach; it translates the case into customer terms, and makes it absolutely clear you are seeing things from their point of view. Check you are doing it justice; all your briefing and much of your thinking about your company and its products/services will be introspective, and may prompt an introspective view and approach, unless you do so.

Tell customers what Is In It for them

Knowing how and why customers view you and your organisation as they do is a prerequisite to improving all the specific communication areas reviewed here and to making your own use of them more effective.

3. Making Ideas Convincing

If benefits are claims for the product/service, they may have to be substantiated, as sales claims are always viewed with some scepticism. This can be done by describing the features which produce them, or by reference to third parties.

Third party references must be used only to support the case, not as arguments in themselves. If a specific third party is named, it should be one respected by the listener (probably not a competitor), and should face similar conditions to the customer. A third party should not just be mentioned, but linked to a description of the particular benefits and need satisfactions that they obtained.

The service industry example that follows shows the correct linked use of the benefits (B) and features (F).

Simple statement B–F

For example, 'You will get more assignments if you use Benefits that match the client's Needs'.

Comparison statement B–F–WA*–NE*

For example, 'You will get more assignments if you use Benefits that match the client's Needs. Vague or unrelated Benefits have a low impact.'

Sandwich statements B–F–WA–NE–F–B

For example, 'You will get more assignments if you use Benefits that match the client's Needs. Vague or unrelated Benefits have a low impact; but by carefully selecting Benefits that have a strong appeal you will get more business and get it sooner.'

*WA – Wrong action
*NE – Negative effect

Obtaining feedback

To ensure that progress is being made towards the ultimate objective, accurate feedback is necessary all the time. It is then possible to be flexible and readjust as the conversation proceeds. By observation, by waiting and listening to the customer's reply, and by asking for a comment, feedback can be assured, at the same time monitoring questions constantly to be answered. Am I discussing your needs? Is this a problem? Is my proposition attractive, clear and convincing? Have I overlooked anything? Whatever is appropriate to ensure that the customer's needs are being satisfied, keep the customer involved in the discussion and prevent problems developing later on.

Presenting one's case is simple and successful if one follows these basic rules:

– take one point at a time;
– tell the client what it means to him in terms of results;
– show him what it is or means;
– provide proof where necessary;
– check progress by obtaining constant feedback.

Obtaining feedback and maintaining a two-way aspect to the conversation (yet maintaining control) is crucial. Some of it is as simple as making sure you listen (again). Pardon? Listen, really listen and use, and be seen to use, the information you are given to tailor your case. Anything else will seem like the 'standard patter'.

So far so good

This stage is clearly crucial. It often constitutes the majority of the sales meeting. It should reinforce all the good initial impressions formed by the prospect in the early stages, particularly:

– professionalism;
– customer orientation;
– technical competence and clear expression;

and, generally, an acceptance that 'this is the sort of person we can do business with'.

This is also the stage where real differentiation develops and can become significant, where the prospect begins to log areas where you are different, and more to his liking than the others. This is also where the detail begins to mount up.

While this will not outweigh a poor product or service, it will augment a good one, and will contribute to the creation of the right balance as the prospect weighs up what he is being offered.

4. Handling objections

This stage is less neat. Objections can occur throughout the whole process, though perhaps most come towards the end of the presentational stage. Some objections are inevitable, a part of the weighing-up process buyers go through in which they search for the plus and the minus points of any proposition put to them. In this sense objections can be a sign of interest.

But there are other more down-to-earth reasons why objections arise that are within a salesperson's control:

– he may not have identified and agreed the customer's needs;
– he may have offered his solutions too soon;
– he may have talked features instead of benefits;
– his benefits may have been too general or too numerous;
– he may have failed to obtain or recognise feedback.

Thus, it has to be said that many objections are not inherent in customers; they are caused by salespeople. You should reduce the frequency and intensity of objections by selling well, but from time to time they will still arise.

How to keep control

So, when they do occur, the first thing to recognise is that most objections have both an emotional and rational content. Emotionally, the customer becomes defensive or aggressive! Rationally, he requires a logical answer to the particular objection that he has raised. To handle them successfully you will need to tackle the emotional and rational aspects separately and sequentially.

We will look first at how to handle the emotional aspect and keep things under control. Its importance can be illustrated by the frequency with which current affairs programmes on radio and TV degenerate into slanging matches. If you watch them closely you will see that the trouble starts when one participant says something with which another disagrees. Instead of controlling their emotions and dealing with the point clearly and logically, they criticise each other. The rest you know only too well.

Keeping control is easy if we put ourselves in the customer's position when he finds disadvantages in a proposition. If we were customers, we would want the salesperson to listen to our point of view, to consider it, and to acknowledge that our point was reasonable – and to do so before he answered. We can do the same with objections raised by customers, keep control, and as a result allow him to consider the answer calmly and rationally.

The conversation might go like this. The customer identifies a 'snag' and voices his objections, 'I think the system will be too complicated for our people and, therefore, they won't use it.'

The salesperson listens; pauses; and acknowledges, 'It probably does look complicated to anyone who hasn't seen it before and we obviously need to take that into account when it's being installed.'

Notice that the salesperson has not yet answered the objection. All he has done is shown understanding of the customer's point of view and met the first point in the buying sequence: 'I am important and want to be respected.'

The diagram in Figure 5.2 shows graphically how this process works. So often, rational answers to objections are less than successful because the customer is emotionally unable to evaluate them fairly. By listening, pausing and acknowledging, we keep the customer's emotions under control and give our answers the best chance of being accepted.

Such holding remarks, as in the example just given, may be quite brief – 'That's a good point', 'We will certainly need to

Figure 5.1 Dealing with objections

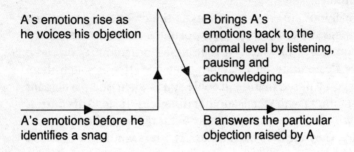

A's emotions rise as he voices his objection

B brings A's emotions back to the normal level by listening, pausing and acknowledging

A's emotions before he identifies a snag

B answers the particular objection raised by A

consider that' – but, despite this, they may serve another purpose. Human design is such that in the time it takes us to say a phrase such as, 'We will certainly need to consider that', there can be a considerable amount of thinking going on. Such remarks give us a chance to consider what we ought to say next. They can be invaluable if the objection has really thrown you (never let it show on your face or in your manner, incidentally).

Before considering how to answer objections, we must point out that you need to understand what the objection means. Never be afraid to answer a question with a question. Alternatively, if the objection comes as a challenge (without a question mark at the end), it may help to turn the objection into a question, and so establish the customer's need behind his resistance. Why is he asking this? Is it an excuse? Delaying tactics? Perhaps he has a point? An apparently straightforward comment such as 'It is very expensive', may mean a wide range of different things from 'It is more than I expected' to 'No', from 'It is more than I can agree' (though someone else might) to 'It is very expensive' and so on. For example, on a recent course, participants I asked to think about alternative meanings for the phrase 'It is very expensive' produced 36 within 10 minutes or so, most necessitating a different answer from each other.

Checking the status of the objection does not mean that we do not have to answer it. We do. Think of objections as minus signs, of different sizes, sitting on the balance the customer is conjuring up in his mind. There are only three ways of dealing with them. Either you explain that the point is not valid, and the balance is therefore more positive, as the point is removed from the minus side; or you persuade them it is less significant than they fear, so most of its weight goes; or you agree (there is no merit in trying to convince them black is white). In all three cases, particularly the latter, the salesperson's response may need to include some re-emphasis on the positive side also.

You have to know your product/service well to produce a good answer. The following approaches will help.

The boomerang

This approach (mentioned on page 19) in the context of tele-phone appointments) pushes the question back to the customer:

C 'I am sure I could get something cheaper.'
S 'There are plenty of models around that are less expensive, it's true. However, you were saying earlier that the minimum level of production rejects cannot be exceeded, and the model we are discussing . . .'

Pre-empting

Here the objection is assumed, avoided and dealt with.

S 'You may well feel this only applies to organisations larger than yours, I would like to show you, however, how it has particular benefits for your kind of firm . . .'

Delay

This is as close as you can get to not answering. In fact, you answer later.

C 'Now, before we get into the detail, I am concerned about the level of training this machine necessitates. Just how long is involved?'

87

S 'That's crucial, of course, I am sure your staff have enough to do already, but it does depend on which model suits you best. Perhaps we can explore that and come back to training.'

Tacit denial

This leaves the point on one side, and concentrates on balancing factors.

C 'The capital cost is too high.'
S 'Well, it isn't the cheapest solution, but the maintenance costs will be less than now and the quality achieved higher.'

Final objections

Here, whatever the query, it is investigated thus.

S 'Apart from delivery, is there anything else you need to be satisfied about before placing an order?'

The customer can then say that everything else is fine, or produce a list to be dealt with. The former remark is particularly useful near to the end of the meeting as a lead into the close.

There is a need to deal promptly and definitely (not glibly) with objections; you have to have the courage of your convictions and sometimes a simple, but sound, answer to seemingly dramatic objections that meets the point head on changes the flow of the conversation. A price objection, 'That's very expensive', met simply with, 'Yes, it is a considerable investment', may be followed by a long pause, after which the prospect moves on to something else.

As a final illustration, we will stay with price objections. Any mechanism which prompts the right response, to any objection in fact, is useful. With price, the following, using the mathematical symbols as a prompt to memory, leads into some good responses:

Sign	The words you should use to emphasise what the price will mean
+ (benefits)	add; added-value; in addition; plus; augment; reinforce; enhance; strengthen; develop.
− (losses)	less; reduce; minimise; contraction; condense; restrict; exclude.
× (productivity)	multiply; considerable; numerous; ample; productivity; performance; majority.
÷ (product cost)	share; divide; proportion; amortise; part; distribute; measure.
= (totality of package)	equal; equivalent; will mean; will produce; total; ultimately; outcome; benefit; results.

SALES EDGE 10 | Handling Objections

- anticipate likely objections
- select and deal with appropriate ones before they are raised
- be seen to respond in a considered manner
- do not be – or at least appear to be – caught out

You should rarely be caught out by objections you have not foreseen, at least in general terms. Thus, handling them effectively is another result of good preparation. There will always be some, however, that demand you are 'quick on your feet'. An apparently unexpected objection, well-handled, can be impressive, and taken as a display of competence.

Use prevention and cure to handle objections effectively

Objections have to be dealt with; but, remember, although 'What are the snags?' is an instinctive part of the buying process, by the time the customer reaches this stage he may be sufficiently attracted by the proposal to pass on without raising objections. It pays to concentrate on resistance prevention rather than resistance cure. Agreement on stated needs, and careful selection and presentation of need-related benefits, reduces both the frequency and strength of resistance.

So far so good

While you do not want to encourage objections, quite the reverse, in fact, objection handling is as much prevention as cure, and you can gain from them.

This occurs primarily in two ways. First, objections provide information, and the better the information available in total, the easier it is to sell. The first information they give is that there is interest, since prospects will not bother with any objections if there is no interest. They also provide information about the focus of interest. What concerns the buyer most? What does he, or does he not, understand? And so on.

Secondly, good objection handling is a display of professional competence and can raise your stock with the buyer. Indeed, some objections are voiced specifically as a test ('Let's see how they handle this!').

So, the professional salesperson minimises objections, but handles the inevitable ones well, professionally, in a way that builds up the image of him and his product or service. A glib answer, evasion, argument or a stunned silence will all lose credibility which, at this stage, should be building up positively and well.

5. Closing

Closing is not really a stage. It is a question and a prompt to customer commitment and action. The first rule about closing is simple. Do it! It is all too easy for closing to be avoided, and with it, of course, the trauma of 'Will he say "no"?'. But a close that is no more than, say, 'Does that tell you all you need at the moment?' – getting a pleasant response like 'Yes, thank you so much for all your help', followed by 'Goodbye' – is not really worthy of the term 'close'.

Note, however, that closing does not only apply to getting the order. We want commitments at many stages, especially in complex sales situations. The prospect may agree to:

– a meeting;
– a demonstration;
– receive samples/literature;
– attend an exhibition;
– another meeting (or formal presentation);
– a written proposal or quotation.

All these, and more – sometimes in a sequence – are steps on the way to the sale and need the commitment gained just as much as with the order at the end of the day.

Obtaining commitment

Knowing that the objective of all selling is to obtain customer commitments often obscures the need to remember how buyers arrive at the point of commitment. They only willingly take buying decisions after they have recognised and felt needs, and are convinced that their needs will be satisfied by implementing the proposal. Thus, the best chance of success lies in doing a good job before they reach the stage of asking themselves 'What shall I do?'.

Attempts to get commitment (closing) without first having created desire for the proposition will normally be seen by the customer as pressure tactics. The bigger the decision, the greater the pressure, and the stronger will be the resistance.

Closing does not cause orders, it merely converts a high desire into orders and low desire into refusals. Even when the desire is high, however, the customer may not volunteer a positive commitment. Similarly, the customer may want to make a commitment, but there are several variations of it, and the salesperson wants one particular kind. It is in these situations that closing skills are valuable; such skills concentrate the buyer's mind on the advantages to be gained from the buying decision itself.

There are certain behaviours, questions and comments indicating a general willingness to buy that can provide 'buying signals', indicating the best moment at which to close. Tone of voice, posture, hesitation, nodding, questions on details, showing acceptance in principle, or comments expressing positive interest are all examples. These can be converted into closes, as long as you are careful not to oversell when the customer wants to make a commitment.

So, whether closing is successful or not is dependent on two things. First, there is everything you have done to date. If the preceding stages have not succeeded in stimulating sufficient interest, or if there are still objections niggling at the interest, then there is little likelihood of closing securing final agreement.

Secondly, the closing question must be put in an appropriate and positive fashion. Thus, although this is the crunch point and can sometimes be avoided because of the unpleasant possibility of getting a 'No', the commitment must actually be asked for; the only question is exactly how it is put. There are various methods. Here are some examples.

Direct request

For example, 'Shall we go ahead then and start getting these improvements in service levels?'

Requests like this should be used where the customer likes to make his own decisions.

Command

For example, 'Install this new system in each regional office. It will give you the information you want much more quickly and help you to make more effective decisions.'

This can be used where the customer:

– has difficulty in making a decision; or
– has considerable respect for the salesperson.

Immediate gain

For example, 'You mentioned that this year the company really needs to improve productivity. If you can give me the go-ahead now, I can make sure that you see specific results within three months' time.'

This could be used where, by acting fast, the customer can get an important benefit, whereas delay might cause him severe problems. The 'hard' version of this is the . . .

Fear close

As in 'Unless you can give me the go ahead . . .'. This is a more powerfully phrased version of 'immediate gain', and should be used with discretion.

Alternatives

For example, 'Both these approaches meet your criteria. Which one do you prefer to implement?'

This could be used where the salesperson is happy to get a commitment on any one of the possible alternatives.

'Best solution'

For example, 'You want a system that can cope with occasional off-peak demands, that is easy to operate by semi-skilled staff and is presented in a form that will encourage line managers to use it. The best fit with all these requirements is our system "X". When's the best time to install it?'

This should be used when the customer has a mix of needs, some of which can be better met by the competition, but which, when taken as a whole, are best met by your solution.

Question or objection

For example, 'If we can make that revision, can you get the finance director to agree to proceed?'

This should be used where you know you can answer the customer's objection to his satisfaction.

Assumption

For example, 'Fine. I've got all the information I need to meet your requirements. As soon as I get back to the office I'll prepare the necessary paperwork and you'll have delivery by the end of next week.'

In other words, we assume the customer has said 'Yes' and continue the conversation on this basis.

Concession

Trade only a small concession to get agreement now or agree to proceed only on stage one.

So far so good, our closing question is slipped in as a natural part of the conversation. It should provide the customer with an appropriate moment at which to confirm his willingness to act. The answer at this point may well be 'Yes'.

No matter how well a presentation is given and questions handled in selling, the prospect may still sometimes have objections to making a decision. Sometimes these are stated, but often they are reserved and come in the form, 'I'll think about it'.

When this happens, simple closes may only irritate the prospect and the way forward may be unclear. Yet it is a key stage to get over, and this can be done by listing the objections, 'I agree you should think about it. However, it's possibly your experience also that when someone says they want to think about it it's because they are still uncertain about some points. In order to help our thinking on these, let's note them down.' Then make a list with room for more objections than he has; do not write any down until each is understood, and do not answer any – yet. Flush them all out and be sure there are not more to come. This enables an additional closing technique to be used, 'If I'm able to answer each of these points to your complete satisfaction, can we

SALES EDGE 11 | Closing

- recognise that everything you do leads up to closing
- watch for 'buying signals'
- close at the right moment
- match closing technique to individual customers

Some of the available business will go to those prepared to tie it down positively. It can be awkward actually to say, 'Right, when do we start?'. Or whatever. This is probably because we know they could say 'No'. But not asking – or saying – 'Please think about it', leaves us open to our more positive thinking competition.

Be positive, watch for, and overcome any psychological fear of closing, and go for it

agree we're in business?'. This is the *conditional close*. Each point listed is answered in turn, crossed off the list, and the prospect's agreement with each checked, then the close is not repeated, but assumption used to conclude matters, 'Fine, now we're in business'.

Having made a commitment, a customer may need reassurance that he has done the right thing. Always thank him, confirm that he has made a wise decision, touch once more on what will come from it, conclude and leave promptly. If you hang about, the customer may start to rethink matters and the good that has been done may start to be undone!

When the customer has been satisfied on the first points in the buying process, a close, emphasising the need satisfaction that a commitment will bring, will naturally convert desire into action.

Good selling can often make formal closing unnecessary, 'Make him thirsty and you won't have to force him to drink'.

Of course, the commitment given may not be to do business. The necessity for 'steps on the way' has been referred to previously, when setting objectives was reviewed. (In Chapter 6 we look, briefly, at the important question of matters that come after the face-to-face meeting, and may apply to additional stages that may be necessary to the customer.)

Finally, there are certain factors that tend to be buyers' 'pet hates', that is they have a disproportionately negative impact, especially if a buyer finds a number of them cropping up in one meeting. So, beware, if you do not get to the point quickly enough, or are too abrupt, you may be in trouble. Similarly, talking too much and not asking enough questions (or asking them, but ignoring the answers); appearing inadequately informed about the product/service, the market or competition (or giving the impression you know it all); interrupting the buyer or ignoring his stated needs or preferences; putting on too much pressure (but equally neglecting to close); displaying a lack of self-confidence (or trying too hard); being scruffy, impolite, whining about the poor market or unfair competition; failing to take an interest in the buyer, his situation or to express any enthusiasm for the whole process; all can create a negative reaction. Any failure to communicate clearly makes things worse.

In all we have reviewed about the face-to-face meeting, individually the elements are really only common sense. There is a good deal to remember, however; a good deal to keep in mind as you actually go through the meeting and attempt to fine-tune what you are doing. And the small details are as important as the overall structure; many a sale must have been won or lost on the inclusion of one extra phrase or more detailed description, or the exclusion of something that dilutes the case. The greatest challenge is perhaps orchestrating the whole process. So, avoid the pitfalls, be particularly aware of those areas of the process that potentially create an edge and your strike rate will be better.

So far so good

In many businesses, if you cannot close, you cannot sell. It is crucial. It must be done positively and in a way that positions it as the natural conclusion to satisfactory discussions.

People may buy from people they do not like, nor even respect, if the product is good enough. However, they are more likely to buy if everything done throughout the meeting says that the salesperson is a professional.

Further, closing sets the scene for a good future relationship; if you help people to buy something with which they are subsequently satisfied, they will come back for more. Today's satisfied customers are tomorrow's best prospects. The salesperson himself is an important part of any decision by the buyer to repeat the experience, or discuss larger requirements for the future.

Regard closing as a beginning, and you will do better in future.

6

Proposals and Formal Presentations – *no weak links*

The ability to express an idea is almost
as important as the idea itself.
Bernard Baruch

However good the salesperson is face-to-face, this still may not
be sufficient to ensure success. Other skills are now an important, and regular, part of the sales process, indeed these often
form a regular part of the cycle of events in some sales situations.
Unless these skills are as good, and as well deployed, as the core
sales skills then there can be no sales edge, and, at worst, the
salesperson may face a real disadvantage.

Two such additional skills are increasingly vital in linking and
completing the process, and are reviewed here by way of example. These skills are written proposals and formal presentations,
and often the two are linked.

We will consider written communication first. In almost any
organisation, if you rate the sales team on a scale of say 1 to 10 for
face-to-face sales skills, and then do so again for written persuasiveness, they will usually rate a couple of points lower.
Sometimes more. Why? Well, in part it is tradition and training.
Salespeople talk to people and written communication is largely
unnecessary; or so says the conventional wisdom. Now it is
becoming more necessary, some simply do not have the expertise
to tackle it effectively.

There is also, if we are honest, a lack of thought. The same arrogance which may encourage a salesperson to run a meeting 'off the top of their head', with no preparation, can have the effect of allowing writing to take place on 'automatic pilot'. When this occurs, too much tends to be a reiteration of a formula for producing a particular kind of letter, proposal or whatever, which, on examination, has little more rationale than being 'the way it has always been done'. In fact, all written communication needs some thought.

This is easily checked. Next time you are in the office pull out from the file the last few things you wrote and posted to customers. Read them through, and try to do so with an objective eye – ask yourself 'would this persuade me. Really?'. If doing this, or even thinking about it, gives you pause for thought, read on.

Letters

Letters last. Unlike telephone calls (which are not often recorded) they stick around to be reread and reconsidered. They need to look neat; think with what trepidation you start reading something that is illegible or untidy.

No matter what the subject of the letter is (and *sales* letters include letters fixing or confirming appointments, introducing yourself, issuing an invitation, even following up after a complaint), you want to be sure that your letters will a) command attention, b) be understood, and c) be acted upon (it is this last that differentiates persuasive communication from simple factual communication). If your letters are to do this, you have to take some care in preparing them; in this age of dictating machines and rush and pressure, it is all too easy to just 'dash them off'.

Preparing persuasive (sales) letters

Before you even draft a letter, remember the sequence of persuasion (see Chapter 4), and in particular remember to try to see things through the other person's eyes. Then ask five questions.

1. For whom is the letter and its message intended? (This is not always only the person to whom it is addressed.)
2. What are their particular needs?
3. How do our ideas or propositions satisfy those needs – what benefits do they give?
4. What do we want the reader to do when he receives the letter? We must have a clear objective for every letter, and these objectives must be clear. (You cannot write the letter, then decide what you want the reader to do; you must write the kind of letter that will best prompt the action you have in mind.)
5. How does the reader take this action?

The last two questions are frequently forgotten, but they are very important. It should be perfectly clear in your own mind what you want the recipient to do, and very often this can be put equally clearly to the reader; but having achieved this, you can lose the advantage if lack of information makes it difficult for them to take the action you want.

The most important part of a letter is the first sentence, or possibly the first two. They will determine whether or not the rest of the letter is read. People seldom read a letter in the same sequence in which it was written. Their eyes flick from the sender's address to the ending, then to the greeting and the first sentence, skim to the last – and then, if the sender is lucky, back to the first sentence for a more careful reading of the whole letter. So the first sentences contain about the only chance you have of 'holding' the reader, and should arouse immediate interest. But gimmicks should be avoided. They invariably give the reader the impression of being talked down to. So how can we achieve the best opening?

Make sure the start of the letter will a) command the reader's attention, b) gain their interest, and c) lead easily into the main text. For example:

- ask a 'Yes' question;
- tell them why you are writing to them particularly;
- tell them why they should read the letter;
- flatter them (carefully);
- tell them what they might lose if they ignore the message;
- give them some 'mind-bending' news (if you have any).

The body of the letter runs straight on from the opening. It must consider the reader's needs or problems from his point of view. It must generate interest. It must get the reader nodding in agreement, 'Yes, I wish you could help me on that'.

And of course you are able to help. In drafting you should write down what you intend for the reader and, of course, list the benefits, not features and in particular the benefits which will help solve that problem and satisfy that need.

You have to anticipate possible objections to your proposition in order to be able to select your strongest benefits and most convincing answers. If there is a need to counter objections, then you may need to make your letter longer and give proof, e.g. something about a third party (the fact that your product is used by a notable company, has won an award or is approved by a technical body, perhaps) selected from the range of such information that should be available. This will reinforce the point and demonstrate that benefits stated are real. However, remember to keep the letter as short as possible.

Your aims should be the following:

- to keep the reader's immediate interest;
- keep that interest with the best benefit;
- win him over with a second benefit (or more);
- obtain action at the end.

In drafting you should make a (short) summary of the benefits of your proposition. Having decided on what action you want the reader to take, you must be positive about getting it. It is necessary to nudge the reader into action with a decisive final comment or question (just as was advocated in Chapter 5 when we looked at face-to-face contact).

A word about language

Remember that your intention is to prompt the customer to action rather than demonstrate your 'Oxford English' (though it is nice to be grammatically correct). You should write much as you speak.

Here are some useful rules: be clear; be natural; be positive; be courteous; be efficient; be personal; be appreciative. In other words, just as we said earlier about language on the telephone. It is perhaps doubly important in writing where a 'civil service' style can all too easily take over. (If this is a weak spot for you, it is worth checking up on; see the next section.)

Throughout the whole process bear in mind exactly who you are going to be communicating with; in other words have their characteristics very much in mind.

Is it someone you know well? Where a good mutual understanding exists you can get straight to the point without too much preliminary.

Is it someone with the same understanding of the topic of discussion as you? In this case no elaborate explanation is necessary.

Is it someone senior, older or more important than you? Someone who will expect, or appreciate, a little respect?

Are they going to be difficult? (Do we know this or are we assuming it?) If so, do we need to be that much more careful, polite or circumspect?

There are few rules here, and most problems occur simply because not enough time and trouble has been taken to think the letter through and adapt your approach to the circumstances.

Reading about writing

There may be no such thing as 'perfect' writing, but most people do it better, and quicker, if what they do is based on some study. Yet this is something that rarely happens. So, although a dissertation about the use of English is beyond the scope of this book, it may be useful at this point to mention one or two references. The following are not only good books, they are interesting, a pleasure to read – or dip into – and are therefore likely to be used.

Keith Waterhouse *English, our English* (Viking 1990) Short, amusing to read, and gives exceedingly good advice.

The Right Word at the Right Time: A guide to the English language and how to use it (Readers Digest 1985) A long reference book, but it is so well arranged, and with so many examples, that it is a pleasure to dip into.

The Good Word Guide (Bloomsbury 1990, Ed. Martin H. Manser) A good paperback guide to spelling, punctuation and grammar in an easy-to-use layout.

If you find writing a chore, you may be surprised how a little research can make it easier.

Proposals

Most businesses need to use persuasive correspondence. Sometimes more elaborate written documentation is involved. The proposal or quotation often comes between one meeting and another, or between a meeting and a presentation. The sequence will vary, but it is always an important link.

The proposal is a tool to help close the sale successfully. By itself, the proposal will not get the order; proposals do not sell, people do, but a good proposal can and must help you to succeed.

A proposal is more complex than a letter, though the principles reviewed over the last few pages are all relevant to proposals. It has to command attention and be understood and should be designed to be acted upon. It must put across any technical information clearly – a process that must be done to match the customer's point of view. Before pen is put to paper it will be necessary to think clearly about the intentions of any specific proposal. For whom is the proposal and its message intended? (This is not always only the person to whom it is addressed.) What are the customer's needs? How does your position satisfy those needs? What benefits does it give?

What do you want the prospect to do when he receives the proposal? Every proposal must have clear objectives:

– it must be commercially worth while;
– it should be stated in terms of customer needs;
– it should be realistic and achievable;
– it must be specific, clear and appropriately timed;
– it must be capable of evaluation with a yes/no answer;
– lastly, how does the prospect take this action?

It is necessary to select a 'shape' for the proposal that will ensure it makes sense to the prospect and can be made persuasive. The proposal must:

– be well organised, with the flow of information easy to follow;
– be put in a logical sequence, so that the prospect will agree each point progressively;
– highlight critical areas of particular interest to the prospect;
– state all the facts that the decision-maker needs;
– summarise all previous agreements;
– be easily understood – by all those who may read it;
– position your organisation in an appropriate role/position.

There are essentially two types of proposal; a letter proposal or a formal proposal. In general, the complexity of the sales situation and the prospect's business methods will be a guide to determining which type of proposal to use.

A letter proposal summarises the critical elements of the recommendations for the decision-maker in letter form. Attachments that document the solution or provide extra information can be added where necessary.

The letter proposal is appropriate when:

– a more detailed proposal is not required;
– recommendations can be clearly presented within the scope of a letter;
– it is necessary only to summarise what has already been agreed upon;
– all prospect concerns are solved;
– there is no competition for the business.

The formal proposal is a more detailed approach to presenting recommendations. A formal proposal is appropriate when:

- recommendations are complex;
- recommendations will be perceived as high in cost;
- the decision-maker is dependent upon recommendations and influencers to help make the buying decision and it is clear that their involvement is important;
- the decision-maker or some of the recommenders and influencers have not met personally;
- there is competition.

Proposal contents

We will now look at the likely sections of a proposal in sequence.

Introduction

Remember that a proposal is a sales document; the opening must command attention, gain interest and lead into the main text. Initial impressions are important, so the first sentence must not be wasted.

In the introduction you need to establish the background, state the purpose of the letter/proposal and refer to previous discussion/agreements.

You can also include a title page (with the customer's name, an index, terms of reference and credits).

Statement of need

This describes the scope of the requirement and makes it clear that the writer understands what is necessary, and how it will be decided upon, and what purchasing criteria are involved.

Ideally, the statement of need does no more than confirm in writing what was originally asked for and added to during earlier visits. It has the value of emphasising the identity of views between the parties, showing the customer that you understand what he wants and does not want from an external supplier.

The more technical a product or service is the more the agreed needs need to be spelt out clearly. Selling a financial service makes a good example. For instance, details of client needs for an audit proposal from an accountant that could be stated individually might include such factors as the following.

- It complies with existing statutory requirements.

- It is unqualified and will satisfy shareholders when published.

- It improves investors' confidence by safeguarding shareholders' interest with an independent viewpoint.

- It helps the client get credit from banks and suppliers.

- It gives him security by having generally accepted accounting principles giving 'correct' financial information.

- It uses control mechanisms proven in his industry, giving him confidence in the production of correct results.

- It shares the burden of audit responsibility, by protecting management while also controlling their audit activity.

- It allows the situation to be under the client's control at all times.

- It gives a minimum of disturbance to his operation and his customers.

- It does not overload staff.

- It avoids the necessity of costly databanks and in-house experience by ready access to the accountant's skills, especially in tax and accountancy.

- It gives information which can be adapted for various user needs, e.g. ownership, management and personnel.

- It gives cost-saving suggestions from familiarity with the organisation, e.g. systems, taxes, etc.

The solution

The solution describes the suggestion not just in terms of technical details (features), but in terms of its advantages and benefits. If possible, it should be made exclusive, i.e. the benefits offered cannot be duplicated by competition.

There is no more effective way to ensure a reader's attention than to make certain that the content of the proposal is totally directed towards him and his needs. Everything the proposal contains must not only be relevant to the prospect, but its relevance must also be explained and he must agree with it.

A standardised or unthought-out approach, may become confusing or present a picture which hardly refers to what was formally established, and certainly does not deal in depth with the prospect's real needs one by one.

It is easier to make these points than to determine how they should be phrased. Advantages must be translated so that the implications are apparent, by using phrases like 'which means that . . .' Features of the approach, method or services are less important than the benefits – what it means or will do for the prospect. Using these factors together in the sequence of setting out benefits first, then linking them to the appropriate features, will present the most powerful argument, and avoid the comment 'So what?'; just as in a meeting.

In addition, reference to timings and delivery can be made at this stage.

Costs

All costs need to be stated clearly, but also related to the benefits of the suggestions, plus any intangible factors.

Quotes must be alive to going rates for similar products/ services, and to the prospect's views and perception of value for money. The prospect must be convinced that he will get value for money. Since some prospects will only read this section, it should start with a short summary of the benefits of dealing with you.

Even if no exact cost is given in the proposal, a range or a top figure may need to be worked out. This is in case of pressure at later meetings, where dissatisfaction may ensue if the prospect receives no indication at all. Do not disguise any costs, but do support them with benefits.

Proceeding to discuss any associated areas, perhaps of manpower, guarantees, training or the implementation timetable may help to move the reader positively away from the costs. It may be useful to amortise costs to illustrate their value (i.e. spread them, £1,000 per month is £12,000 amortised across the year).

Closing statement

This can refer to any attachments, for example, appendices/ technical specifications/literature or samples. It should create a sense of urgency, so that the decision-maker will act promptly and should close, i.e. ask for the commitment, making it clear what the next action is to be.

A summary of why this proposal is right will help those key executives who are very busy and who need a precise statement of the facts to help them make a decision, and those key personnel for whom the proposal is the only contact if they were not present at meetings or presentations. Repeating the benefits after the costs section means that a reader is left with a final impression of the benefits rather than just the price.

Such a summary might include a review of the origin and scope of research effort, an outline of the key findings on what is wanted, and a summary of what is offered and how that meets the prospect's criteria for external support. It might finish with a summary of tangible and intangible benefits.

Proposal format

In a formal proposal, each section should have its own page, a table of contents will make it clearer and the letter accompanying the proposal (if it is posted rather than presented) must not be a formality, but should add something to the case itself – perhaps strengthening urgency or specifying further action, for example:

- you might give an appreciation of being asked to quote, reassuring the prospect that he was right in contacting the firm;

- you might emphasise that the proposal represents the mutual conclusions of the prospect and the proposer;

- you could close by indicating who can be contacted, or promising to contact in the near future, and suggesting a timetable of action.

Style and language are important too. The document should be attractively laid out, grammatically correct and well typed. It should look formal, efficient, individual and clear.

Layout

Layout is especially important: the proposal should not be squeezed into one, two or any particular number of pages. Headings and paragraphs will ensure clarity and emphasis; <u>underlining</u>, or CAPITALS or **bold type** may help you get the attention you want.

<u>As may indenting, and perhaps</u>
<u>emphasising a key sentence or point.</u>

All the suggestions for writing good letters apply equally to proposals; more so in fact, in view of their greater length.

Proposals are important, time-consuming and too often a weak link. Have a look at the last few that have gone out from your own firm, check that you are really happy that they do a persuasive job and, if they need fine-tuning, give your future proposals just a little more thought.

The checklist in Figure 6.1 can be used either to help you compose a suitable proposal, or to see how a past one is likely to have been regarded.

Figure 6.1 **Proposal Checklist**

1. *Have you selected the appropriate proposal format?*

Letter proposal

Yes   No
☐   ☐   Can you adequately present your recommendation in a letter with attachments?
☐   ☐   Is it agreed that you need merely to summarise what you discussed/agreed?
☐   ☐   Are all prospect concerns resolved?
☐   ☐   Has competition been eliminated?

Formal proposal

☐   ☐   Are your recommendations complex?
☐   ☐   Will your recommendations be perceived as high in cost?
☐   ☐   Do you want to demonstrate the involvement of recommenders and influencers upon whom the decision-maker will rely in making the buying decision?
☐   ☐   Will you be unable to meet with the decision-maker or with other key recommenders or influencers?

2. *Do you know who may influence the decisions to buy?*

☐   ☐   Decision-maker?
☐   ☐   Recommenders?
☐   ☐   Influencers?
☐   ☐   Others? _____

_____

3. *Does your proposal contain the following?*

Does the introduction include
☐   ☐   A background statement?
☐   ☐   The purpose of the proposal?
☐   ☐   An emphasis on mutual conclusions?

Does the statement of need include
☐   ☐   Clear and specific enumeration of needs directly related to recommendations?
☐   ☐   The scope of the problem?
☐   ☐   A statement of the prospect's decision criteria?

Does the solution include
- ☐ ☐ A list of recommendations?
- ☐ ☐ The relationship of recommendations to needs?
- ☐ ☐ A statement of how recommendations meet the prospect's decision criteria?
- ☐ ☐ The features, advantages and benefits of your products and services?

Does the closing statement include
- ☐ ☐ A summary of the tangible benefits?
- ☐ ☐ An identification of intangible benefits?
- ☐ ☐ An amortisation of costs where appropriate?

Does the closing statement include
- ☐ ☐ A description of attachments?
- ☐ ☐ A statement urging prompt and specifically stated action?

Have you included the appropriate attachments/samples?
- ☐ ☐ Samples?
- ☐ ☐ Descriptive brochures?
- ☐ ☐ Others? _____

_____

Comments: _____

_____

_____

_____

In summary, never let the written word become a weak link. The quality of what goes out to customers, whether it is a three line letter or a thirty page proposal, must be good. It should be seen as reflecting the good impression already made at meetings, it should stand out from what may be received from competitors, and above all, it should be factually clear and provide the required and appropriate information. Customers should feel it adds to their ability to make a sensible, considered decision.

Written communication may also link in sequence to the next topic we review, forming a basis of any presentational stage.

Presentations

There are, of course, different kinds of presentation. Some may be promotional, perhaps an opportunity to address a conference or a spot during promotional events, often called 'client seminars'. Some are speculative, such as the 'beauty parade' when the presentation comes first in the cycle of sales events. Others are the last stage in the series of events.

All of these can make you vulnerable.

In every case your competence is on display, and the quality of everything from your delivery to your future after-sales service is judged, in part, directly on the effectiveness of your presentation. People do not say 'that was a poor presentation', but 'I think that is an unsuitable supplier'.

Here we will take a follow-up presentation as an example. So, we will assume that there has been a meeting, that written proposals have been submitted and now the next meeting is being held to present the content, formally, to a group at the customer's premises, maybe the board, maybe a committee.

It is beyond the scope of this book to review every aspect of presentational skill, though it should be noted that it is a skill, and one that (almost) everyone can develop to some degree with some training. The essentials are worth a moment however, and to do this we will go back just a little in the sequence.

Proposals, however good they are, can only do so much on their own. They need follow up, backing up – another meeting, a presentation. Or the presentation format may be something the customer specifies; something that appears to be happening more often. In some industries inherent changes – the group practices that medical representatives so often have to sell to now, for instance – make it a necessary, and now regular, event. Rather than have the proposal as the last stage (one at which we are not present), we may want to organise a presentation to ensure another contact.

The moment to agree this, to sell it, is at the end of the previous meeting. Finding out how many copies of the proposal document are needed (which may also provide additional information about the decision-makers) and setting a date, time and perhaps other details (attendance, location) will allow you to plan for the meeting that will best help secure the business.

The ability to make effective presentations is an essential skill, not only in selling to prospects, but also for in-house selling at internal meetings. However, it is an unnatural social act for most people, made more difficult by everyone's familiarity with the polished television performances they see every night.

In addition, many presentations are further complicated by the customer trying to follow a proposal while listening to the presenter explaining something different. The objective of the presentation must be to:

– present the facts, clearly and understandably;
– get feedback, avoid monologue and gain agreement;
– present the case credibly to convince them; and
– be able to answer questions and objections satisfactorily.

So the next Sales Edge concerns writing persuasively.

SALES EDGE 12 | Writing Persuasively

- be as persuasive in writing as you are face-to-face
- take time to get it right
- draft and redraft until satisfied
- make the look as good as the content

If you are good face-to-face do not let letter writing be a weak link. Prevailing standards are not so high, and this makes it a clear opportunity to differentiate yourself from less professional competition.

Make it read like you would want to make it sound

It is not enough, however, just to get it down on paper; as well as being read it must be used.

Using the proposal

The presenter should prepare his copy of the proposal with notes, examples and headlines to guide his talk. Since competitors will be saying mostly the same things (for example, 'we pride ourselves on our good service and technical excellence'), and because just reading the proposal is not enough, it must be turned into an aid to presentation.

As has been said, it is beyond the scope of this book to review every aspect of making a presentation; however, key elements of the presentation process will now be briefly commented on, in sequence.

Present clearly

You should take a structured lead by suggesting a format and timetable for the meeting, for example, that you go through the proposal together with discussion after each subject and a cut-off time in an hour.

You should also hand out and show briefly the contents of the proposal, but suggest that it will be more productive if you study it together, section by section, starting by ensuring that you have the facts right.

You should also follow the proposal, making it clear if you are departing from the sequence in which it is set out, and why, and even reading key sections or summaries out loud to reinforce a key point precisely.

Visual aids

In more formal presentations you may need prepared slides. If so, use prepared aids as visual paragraph markers for ideas. The visuals should sort and emphasise points, *supporting* what you say rather than taking it over. Slides should not include too many words on each one, they should be recognisably a set – that is the same style, colours and layout, and introduced in an organised way; put it up, talk to it, remove it to prevent distraction.

In addition, at any presentation, remember that you are, in effect, a visual aid; how you appear, how you come over, influences the overall effect you produce. So:

– be enthusiastic – if you are not convinced, they will not be;
– stand or sit upright, but vary your position regularly;
– use hands to emphasise rather than distract;
– look at individuals and change expression; and
– vary voice pitch, tone and pace to produce emphasis.

Similarly, you must ensure that the language you use enhances what you say, and develops and holds interest. So:

– use questions as well as statements;
– use metaphors, similes and analogies;
– use examples to paint pictures;
– repeat and summarise frequently before, during and after.

Remember that the proposal is the main aid; it is wasteful to reinvent the wheel.

Present credibly

The first thing to bear in mind here is that a presentation may suffer from trying to be all things to all people. It must be directed specifically, ideally to the decision-maker, and say so. You need to ask yourself questions to ensure that the most appropriate style of delivery is adopted. For instance: who will you address and how will others in the group be brought in? Will you use a formal stand-up or low-key discussion style? Will there be a greater or lesser involvement of others – (perhaps a technical expert) – a team presentation? Will there be a liberal or selective use of aids? Will you make use of customer language/ jargon?

The presentation is the occasion when the prospect and his team are able to judge the human side of your case. They will be using the opportunity to assess your complete capability for:

– doing what you have said;
– doing it better than competitors.

If necessary you must pick your team and agree roles, so that there is no confusion during the meeting. Deciding exactly who attends from your side, and how many, is important, as is the link between that and who will do what thereafter.

Give proof:

– build up credibility;
– demonstrate how your firm has been successful in the past;
– allow individual experience to shine (without boasting);
– use expressions like 'in our experience . . .';
– work in examples of how you have dealt with similar situations;
– illustrate your argument with cases, examples, anecdotes;
– quote convictions and agreements already made by the prospect; and
– above all, talk throughout in terms of benefits.

Feedback

Even a presentation, when, by definition, you will do most of the talking, must remain two-way and avoid becoming a tedious monologue.

During the presentation check for feedback by continually involving the prospects, to get their agreement before moving on; get them nodding early on, by referring to the situation and to matters clearly agreed:

– watch faces and body movements for reactions;
– ask questions to ensure agreement on the need to introduce each main point;
– do not move on if people are still worried;
– summarise frequently;
– make notes of points of agreement and disagreement; and
– watch the time (an accurately timed session is, itself, impressive).

Overall as you plan the presentation:

- ensure that the decision-maker and all his advisers are present;
- ensure that they are pre-sold and looking forward to your presentation;
- avoid presenting anything new that may create resistance;
- emphasise the points that have already been agreed with the decision-maker and his advisers;
- reinforce your message with simple, graphic visuals.

SALES EDGE 13 | Formal Presentations

- recognise that it is 'different on your feet'
- prepare, and give it sufficient time
- practise and rehearse
- make it professional
- add a touch of finesse

It is all too possible for poorer products and services to be bought in preference to better alternatives simply because they are better presented. Presentational standards are higher today than ever before; and professional presentation, on television for instance, increases people's expectations.

This is an area where, while awareness and self-study help, there is no substitute for training. The kind of course, usually using video-recording equipment, which allows you to see how you come over and practise exactly what you do in a way that involves constructive critique, is invaluable, and will act to improve the standard of what is done for (almost) everyone.

Make it clear they are dealing with a professional

Proposals represent the summation of your efforts to date with this prospect, and the commitment to him. This does not mean that large amounts of information should be submitted just to look impressive, but that it should be carefully thought out and well organised.

A well-prepared and presented proposal increases the prospect's confidence (essential when selling intangible services) and increases the possibility of success.

The need for formal presentation at this stage is increasing as customers become more and more inclined to check every aspect of a potential supplier very carefully. It is a key element in differentiating competitors one from another, and one that may demand some training within the firm. So spend time improving, if necessary, your presentational skills and remember that it is all too possible for a poorer, but better presented case, to prompt purchase in preference to a better, but less well-presented, one.

If all these methods are handled as well, with as much attention to detail, and as persuasively as face-to-face meetings, then the basis for a good success rate in pulling down the business will be secured.

If you can be as professional 'on your feet' as across the desk, you create another real edge.

7

Persistence and Follow Up –
keeping in touch

If at first you don't succeed, try, try, again,
Then quit, no use being a damn fool about it.
W.C. Fields

It is said that there are two kinds of people in the world: those who divide the world into two kinds of people; and the rest. Certainly it is simplistic to say that there are two kinds of customer, but in terms of follow up it works quite well.

The first category of customers are those that are, almost by definition, called on regularly. This means where you set a call frequency (the minimum you judge will hold and develop their business effectively) and stick to it; calling, say, once a month. With these, provided an appropriate frequency is set, stuck to and reviewed regularly, there will be little problem.

However, the second category are those customers where ongoing decisions are necessary to maintain contact and develop and maximise business, where the overall frequency of contact has to be planned.

The first rule is to do just that. Persistence is, *per se*, going to make a difference. You have to plan and think about follow up, and steel yourself to make those awkward calls – when you have put in a proposal for instance, or had a successful first meeting, and you must telephone to initiate the next stage. The prospect is busy, out or unavailable. Most of us become paranoid after a couple of such calls. Some quickly give up on it, assuming that there is no merit in continuing contact.

Be warned. Some business goes, quite simply, to those who are more persistent than others; those who keep in touch and are still there when there is business to place. This applies first to the initial sequence of events. Here are some examples.

- Calls to set up an appointment; several may need to be made before you get through. Several may be planned. You may need to make one to discover the name of the decision-maker, another to his secretary to see when he might be available, others to him to try to agree a meeting.

- Calls after a meeting, to arrange the next stage, whether that is another meeting, a proposal, a presentation or a demonstration.

- Calls while a proposal is being considered.

And so on. It is perfectly possible that 'in a meeting', 'busy', 'not here today', 'out of town' and all the other off-putting excuses mean exactly what they say. He *is* busy, out of town, or whatever. Of course, making such calls can be awkward, but only psychologically so.

Other kinds of follow up may also be necessary. Write to them at such stages; a letter is a more permanent reminder of what you hope will happen next than a transient phone call. Better still, use the two together. A letter saying you will call; a letter saying you have called; and touching again on the benefits.

Make more of these kinds of contact than your competitors, and, almost automatically, everything else being equal, you will sell more.

The process should also be longer term. There is a need to keep in touch with customers and others, especially in businesses where their need for your product or service is, by the nature of it, not continuous. In one company I discovered a system they referred to as the LYBUNTs. It stood for 'Last year, but unfortunately not this', and in fact described a system designed to prevent past prospects/customers falling into this category. Any trick that acts as a reminder and makes more happen, more certainly, is useful.

A Follow-Up System

A system to help plan and then ensure follow up takes place is essential. First, consider the actions you can take that will provide 'Keep-in-touch' opportunities. For example you can:

- visit them (a face-to-face meeting may be best, but not every 5 minutes);
- telephone;
- write;
- write and send something (information, a newsletter, press cuttings, an article reprint, advance notice of something, samples, ideas, literature);
- introduce someone else (someone more technical, more senior);
- ask them something (advice, information, an opinion);
- invite them to something (coffee, lunch, dinner, an event or exhibition).

You may well be able to think of more things you can do. Then plan and record a series of actions. This does not necessitate an elaborate system, but it does need a diary (preferably a loose-leaf one so that you always have one system for the next few months) and, perhaps (at least for the most important customers on your territory) a form.

Such a form (an example is given in Figure 7.1), which should be tailored to your needs, can record key details of the customer in the top half and a timed plan of sales action on the bottom. The latter is *not* a record (though it becomes one), it is there to help schedule what should be done ahead and flag what should happen *next*. Only by having it on one sheet like this can the frequency and gaps be shown clearly. A corresponding entry in the diary will make sure each thing happens at the right time.

Figure 7.1 Customer review form

To: _____ From: _____

Ref No: _____

Customer: _____

Address: _____

_____ Tel.No: _____

Contacts

1. Name _____ Position _____

2. Name _____ Position _____

3. Name _____ Position _____

Type of organisation _____

Buying record _____

_____

_____

_____

Comments: _____

_____

_____

Follow-up action

Date:

This may involve a long lead time. I have entries in my diary for a year ahead, but it is not time-consuming to use. It prompts the action. For your bigger customers this may need to relate to the longer-term strategy, and for the biggest this is something that is worth working out in detail. This will be the subject of Chapter 8.

A Reason for Calling

Sales managers often talk of one entry they find on salespeople's reports as being a nonsense; it is the comment (usually under 'Reason for contact') which says 'Courtesy call'. They are right to say this. There is, or should be, no such thing as a courtesy call.

You always need a reason for calling. A good reason. Whether *you* feel it is a good idea, or if there has been a long gap in communications, is irrelevant to the customer. (Another reason I hate is when people say 'I am in your area', which seems to be suggesting that I fit in with the salesperson rather than that they should plan something of interest to me.) A 'good reason' means a good reason in customer terms. If you can say to yourself, 'I am calling today Mr Customer, because . . .', you should be able to follow it with something they will see as a good reason.

In addition, consider the personal relationship between the buyer and seller. This is important. It is not necessary to form a close friendship, though this sometimes happens, but you do need to get on in terms of professional respect. The informal aspects contribute to this. However, there are dangers, which the following apocryphal story makes clear.

A salesman is asked why he achieves such good results with one particular customer. 'It is the personal relationship', he explains. 'We get on well and I am at pains to take an interest in his interests. He is a keen golfer and as long as I always remember to ask how his game has been, enquiring how he got on in the weekend competition, and so on, the relationship is maintained and I go on getting the orders.' The customer is then asked why he continues to deal with the salesman. 'He's a professional', he answers. 'Knows his stuff, is reliable and makes sure his company deliver. I wish there were more like him – just one thing though, I wish he wouldn't waste so much time talking about my golf.'

This story illustrates the difficult line you need to tread. Work insufficiently hard at the relationship and you lose the customer, overdo it and you run the danger of becoming a time waster. An appropriate amount of 'chat', as well as a good reason for being in touch, and you are well on the way to success. Let the chat become, or seem to become, the reason for calling and it may lead to trouble. Again, the moral is to attend strictly to the customer's needs.

Cut Your Losses

Time is one of your most valuable commodities. So, to finish this chapter, we must consider whether there are limits to persistence. After all most acorns do not turn into giant oak trees, they rot in the ground. Experience helps you to spot the good leads, the prospects that have genuine potential, and sometimes this is a long-term situation. Some years ago I remember maintaining contact for $2^1/_2$ years with a major organisation in Hong Kong (partly, I suppose, because of its location), while colleagues pronounced it 'a waste of time'. Then it produced a sizeable piece of business, and became a regular client for some years.

Everyone will doubtless have such examples, but we probably also have recollections of those – and there may well be more of them – that came to nothing. At some point we have to put things on one side and deploy our time and effort on other things.

This does not mean that you forget them. Regular follow up gives way to a name moving to a mailing list perhaps, and receiving an annual newsletter. Occasionally we can go through such lists and re-contact certain, selected contacts.

This can even work to spell out to prospects that you will not now follow up any more – on more than one occasion such a letter has produced an immediate response, perhaps after a long period of silence, saying something like 'Keep in touch' or 'In three months we *will* be ready to talk about this'.

SALES EDGE 14 | **Persistence**

- be very persistent
- keep in touch
- judge the right frequency of contact
- vary the method of contact
- make ongoing contact useful to the prospect

This is simply stated. Keep in touch with the right people, in the right way, at the right frequency and keep on doing so when others have fallen by the wayside. It makes a difference.

Be there when others have given up

Be genuinely objective about this area: keep on trying with the appropriate ones; deploy the time away from the no-hopers towards better opportunities; keep on prospecting to provide 'new blood' for your prospect list; take a long view of follow up, and you will do better than those who give up too soon.

After-Sales Service

As an afterword to this chapter, consider a key long-term implication of follow up; that of after-sales services. As I prepared the manuscript of this book, my office photocopier broke down. I telephoned the supplier, a distributor for the make in question. They were abrupt, unhelpful and wanted what I considered to be an outrageous call-out charge, paid in advance, before they would even come and look. They would not even consider the idea of the small, desk-top machine being brought to them.

So I rang another dealer, actually much nearer my office. They were very helpful, pleased to look at it if it was dropped in – and assured me they would quote before doing any work. So the machine went there mid morning. A call came through within an hour with an estimated cost. By mid afternoon I had a call to say it was ready for collection. The cost? Less than half the first firm's call-out charge. This is not just an example of cost saving, though that is important, but also of service.

Now who is most likely to get my future business? No contest. And it is not just a question of one small photocopier; the firms concerned deal with a wide range of office equipment, so the successful one now has a number of opportunities for the future.

For salespeople this kind of situation may be difficult to influence (though you may need to try to do so), but is one which will certainly affect their likelihood of success. (I know what I shall say if a representative of the first firm follows up with me.) On the other hand, we must not be negative. Maybe the sales team can influence this kind of thing, certainly the sales manager should be able to do so. If not, the answer may be only to take on a sales job in an organisation with good back-up service.

8

Major Sales – *different in nature and in scale*

A wise man will make more opportunities than he finds.
Francis Bacon

Throughout this book emphasis has been put on the need to deal with customers individually and even to vary approaches meeting by meeting. The reader should not assume however that, while the approach needs fine-tuning, customers are in other ways similar. This is not so, and this chapter reviews an area of significant difference. Your larger customers are different in nature as well as size. There is a great deal hanging on getting the relationship with major customers right. Pareto's law, the 80/20 rule, means that a small number of customers are likely to be producing the majority of sales. This is true for companies and for an individual sales territory.

It is not just a question of numbers, however; buying power may be concentrated in fewer hands in many industries, but buying decisions are also being made at higher levels, by more professional buyers who are well equipped to give every supplier's offering detailed scrutiny.

At the same time sales forces are tending to get smaller, and back-up or support staff may not be of a strength to give salespeople all the necessary support. Thus, dealing with major customers demands that there are no weak links, and there is a responsibility in certain key areas if the chances of success are to be increased. These include:

- systematic planning for obtaining, keeping and expanding major accounts;
- identifying and exploiting productive opportunities;
- establishing a business partner relationship with the customer;
- strict monitoring of the activities that lead up to the major sale;
- demonstrating bottom-line solutions to customers' needs.

Thus, major account management is a more complex process than making a one-off sale or general account selling. Basic face-to-face selling skills only form a part of the range of skills required. If they are to make the best use of them, salespeople must have detailed operational and financial knowledge of the customer's business, while their manager may well want to be able to answer 'yes' to the following questions about their salespeople.

- Do they identify as many new major opportunities as we would like?
- Do they qualify major sales opportunities early and easily?
- Do they identify a customer's specific business problems and priorities?
- Do they present our products and services as specific need satisfactions?
- Do they calculate and demonstrate how our products and services can increase sales, and reduce or avoid costs?
- Do they write and present clear, financially-sound proposals?
- Do they close as many major sales as we need?
- Do they build continuing relationships with major customers to minimise competition and assure additional business?

To ensure that all these things do happen, companies want a practical and predictable process that makes the most economic use of sales time, guides and supports salespeople in the lead up to the sale, and provides them with the ammunition to be 'valuably different' from the strongest competitor.

Checklists

It is with these objectives in mind that the checklists summarising the process in this chapter have been prepared. Specifically, they will cover:

- selecting and analysing key opportunities;
- financial analysis of major prospects;
- preparing sales strategies for major prospects;
- cost-justifying solutions to customers' needs;
- planning and conducting sales negotiations;
- expanding major accounts.

Creating a major sale is a time-consuming activity for salespeople, support staff and often top management as well. Therefore, it is important to assess early in the sales cycle which prospects present the best opportunities.

For example, a company selling industrial adhesives and applicators found that one of its sales engineers had spent 3 weeks trying to solve the technically and socially interesting problem of fixing an Adam fireplace in a stately home, instead of pursuing a commercially vital but technically undemanding enquiry from a major prospect. When asked to comment on why this important lead had not been followed up, he replied that he had been 'too busy'. This salesman should have adjusted his priorities.

Selecting and analysing key opportunities

Since the ultimate goal is to add value to the prospect's business, it is also necessary to determine in which areas he seeks improvement. This can be done by understanding his own industry, studying his particular operations and future goals.

- What methods do we have for establishing early on whether there is an obvious need for our products or services in an account?

- If criteria are laid down, are they communicated to the sales force, and monitored by the sales management?

- How are prospects investigated to ensure that eventually they will buy a significant amount of the product service?

- To what extent is the stability of prospects evaluated?

- How do we check that the use of our products or services can be cost justified from a prospect's point of view?

- What effect will the complexity of a prospect's business have on the amount of time we will have to invest?

- How does the long-term potential of a prospect compare with others we might pursue?

- What analysis of a prospect's buying history with us or other suppliers should be carried out to determine whether the opportunity is worth while?

- What ranking of opportunities is done so that priority prospects can be determined?

- How much should we know about the industries to which they belong? How much do we know?

- How well do we know the objectives of the industry to which the prospect belongs?

- Are we aware of the concerns and problems that are specific to that industry?

- How well do we understand the structure of the industry to which the prospect belongs?

- To what extent is the prospect's industry subject to national and local government regulations? Is our sales force aware of them, and their impact on the prospect's need for our products and services?

- Are our sales force and support functions familiar with the specific industry terminology used by the prospect?

- Many sales staff who have a gift for interpersonal relations find it difficult to apply themselves to the analysis and planning necessary for a major sale. Have we:

a) specified the information that must be obtained on every major prospect?
b) created a standard format by which it can easily be collected and presented?
c) trained the sales force in why and how it should be used?
d) ensured that sales management monitors it regularly?

- What is the state of repair of our information collection and analysis system on major prospects?

- Where does the responsibility lie for collecting, analysing and presenting background information on target industries and prospects?

- If individual salespeople are responsible, are they aware of useful published sources of information?

- Do they use them?

- Can they interpret the prospect's own information, such as the annual report?

- If sales intelligence is the responsibility of an internal department, are the staff regularly advised on what to look for and where to find it?

- What priority is given to pre-contact analysis compared with face-to-face selling skills?

- How much time is being wasted on non-opportunities?

- How much business is being lost through lack of pre-contact analysis?

Financial analysis of major prospects

Major customers and prospects are not 'like small ones, only bigger'. As has been noted, they are different in nature as well as in scale and will often require a totally different approach if both volume and profit targets are to be achieved.

The first stage in implementing such an approach is to have an overall policy towards major account business, covering such questions as the following.

- What is our current customer mix?
- How has it come about?
- Was it planned or did it simply happen?
- Was it the right mix?
- Do we have too many customers costing too much to service, or too few customers exposing us to an unacceptable risk?
- Are other mixes possible?
- What sort of mix is desirable?
- What mix will keep costs to a minimum without creating an unacceptable risk?
- What sort of mix will be desirable in 5 or 10 years and what will be the effect on profitability?

More than one supplier, having calculated that they were supplying certain customers on uneconomical terms, has decided to approach the customers to renegotiate terms. One such, armed with detailed analyses of turnover, product mix, sales and servicing costs and comparisons with other customers of a similar size, arranged a meeting with the chief buyer and his team. Meticulously he presented his case, concluding with the statement that current levels of branch calling would have to be reduced, and waited for the buyer's reply. The buyer paused for a moment and then said: 'We wondered how long it would take you to get round to that'.

Having developed an overall policy, companies will often have to take action in two directions: improve the profitability of existing major customer business; and acquire profitable new business from new customers. Action along these lines will inevitably have implications for the company's organisation structure, information systems and selling skills.

To improve major customer profitability, therefore, it is necessary to know how profitable they are at present. The question is, what is meant by customer profitability? How is it measured? And how should the information be presented so that salespeople and others can use it?

Increasingly, companies feel that since the profit and loss account reflects overall company profitability, and since a few major customers can dramatically affect it, they must measure the net profitability of each major customer after deducting all costs directly incurred in supplying, selling and servicing.

Profitability analysis is, of course, only one side of the diagnostic coin. Equally important is the qualitative aspect of the relationship between major supplier and major customer. How, for example, do the various decision-makers and influencers within the customer's organisation rate the supplier *vis-à-vis* the competition in terms of product/service quality, price and terms, and general pre- and post-sales support? What are their priorities in these areas and whose view carries strength? Once this information has been gathered it is comparatively easy to draw up individual major account strategies and action plans to be implemented by the national accounts sales team.

In the following checklist attention is turned to a financial analysis of the prospect so that the appropriate sales strategy can be developed. Two interrelated factors make such an analysis essential.

First, the prospect will almost certainly be faced with the same economic realities as the supplier – pressure on margins, unused capacity, low pre-tax profits and a lack of finance for growth. Consequently, the prospect will be carrying out a much deeper cost/benefit analysis of his own expenditure and, whenever possible, postponing or eliminating entirely any decisions on 'frill's'. Those decisions which are taken will be taken at a higher level than before, probably by board members, in the case of major purchases.

Secondly, what is a major sale for the supplier will probably be a major purchase decision by the customer. It is, therefore, vital that the salesperson handling this account recognises the importance of carrying out a financial analysis of the prospect and has the ability to use the information they obtain. This ability must not simply be confined to cost-justifying recommendations to the buying department, but must also cover any function that has an interest in the decision – production, marketing, finance personnel.

Unfortunately, even senior salespeople are often financially naïve, or top management mistakenly believe that either its salespeople do not need financial skills in order to sell or, worse, that for dubious security reasons they should be kept ignorant of internal costs, margins, costing systems and break-even quantities. Inevitably, in such circumstances, salespeople are handicapped in their ability to negotiate the terms and conditions of the contract after agreement in principle has been reached.

This does not necessarily mean that you should know enough about finance to be able to talk on equal terms with a finance director, but you do need to know enough to be able to spot opportunities and exploit them for the good of both parties. If you do not have the background details you need from your own organisation, you must ask for them.

It is against this background that you should read the following checklist. Its aims are to help improve the management of major account business and to help salespeople gather information on major prospects in a systematic way so that they can prepare their sales strategy and cost justify their proposals to the customer's satisfaction.

Existing major customers

- Have we defined what we mean by a major customer? For instance, 'any customer whose loss would expose us to an unacceptable risk'.

- What proportion of our total business are major customers now taking – individually and as a group?

- Do we know how business from major customers has changed in the past 5 years?

- Are we satisfied with the trends in our customer mix?

- Do we have a policy on customer mix?

- If not, what could be the implications of not having one?

- Do we know how profitable each major customer is?

- How do we measure individual customer profitability?

- Which costs are included in analysing individual customer profitability?

- Have all direct costs, both fixed and variable, been identified?

- Will they vary by customer?

- How does the profit from major customers compare with overall company profit?

- How does the profit from major customers affect overall company profit?

- How does the profit from individual major customers in a particular segment compare with others in the same segment?

- How does the profitability of major customer segments compare?

- What benefits would derive from knowing the profitability of major customers?

- Who currently receives customer profitability information, and who should receive it?

- How do those who receive it use it? Does it provide the database for strategic marketing decisions, individual customer strategies and negotiating objectives?

- Have the following groups been trained to use it? Product/ brand managers, segment managers, market research staff, DP staff, national accounts managers, special accounts salespeople, distribution managers.

- Is customer profitability information presented to them in such a way that they are motivated to use it?

Major prospects

- What financial knowledge should we have on major prospects which will help us understand their goals and plan our strategies?

- Have we developed any system for financial analysis of major prospects and is such a system used?

- Dó we, as a matter of routine, examine a prospect's current financial status and review key categories such as sales, cost of goods sold, gross profit, operating expenses, pre-tax profit?

- Are comparisons made with previous years to identify trends or major changes to see if they offer us sales opportunities?

- When considering major prospects do we extract key ratios in their financial performance and compare them with industry averages to reveal specific needs for our products and services? Check return on capital employed, return on sales, sales on capital employed, productivity per employee, stock turn, debtors, ratio, liquidity, ownership.

- What use is made of standard sources of industry information?

- Are the staff responsible for generating major prospect business able to interpret financial information? Can they read a set of published accounts and relate the figures to the company's products or services?

- Are our senior sales staff aware of our own financial goals in sufficient detail to be able to identify the most valuable opportunities within a prospect's operation?

- Who is responsible for conducting financial analysis of major prospects and the industries to which they belong?

- If it is the responsibility of marketing support staff, what formal methods exist for communicating the information to the sales team?

- Does the sales team have the ability and confidence to discuss a prospect's financial situation and needs?

Preparing sales strategies for major prospects

If an attempt is made to identify the contributors to success in major sales situations, it is often found that two sets of conditions are having to be coped with simultaneously. At the same time, selling is becoming more complex – financially, technically and organisationally. In some industries, the pace of technological change is almost faster than the ability of salespeople to absorb it. In most industries, it is easy to come across people who have the power to say 'No', but difficult to identify the one person who can say 'Yes'.

On the other hand, improvements in market research techniques and a sharp increase in competition have created near parity in product and price offerings in many fields, so that the emphasis falls more and more on presentational and service aspects. This means that marketing people in general, and senior sales staff in particular, have to be far more creative in exploiting marginal variations in product and price, and to become 'interestingly different' to potential customers (this is not, of course, limited to large customers).

This means that salespeople have to obtain data from within the prospect company. They also have to integrate their information-gathering effort with their selling activities which, for ultimate success, will involve several levels of management in different departments. And they need a structure that will make it easy to plan and control the whole process, starting with the initial contacts and finishing with the implementation of the signed order.

This last point needs to be emphasised, since there is plenty of evidence to suggest that the biggest weakness among sales staff in generating and maintaining major sales is often to be found in the absence of structured planning. The reasons for this are obvious.

Psychological barriers to detailed planning are inherent in many sales staff, who have high levels of empathy but literally find it difficult to do analytical work. There is often communication failure between functional departments: 'We and production hate one another's guts, but the common enemy is accounts', who need to collaborate to meet customers' needs.

By having a structured system, you will find it easier to organise your time and effort to obtain the information to make your solutions interestingly different in the customer's eyes, to impress prospects with your efficiency, to co-ordinate the resources of your own company and to keep your own manager informed.

This structured system, which covers the entire sales strategy, will normally include these elements:

- identifying key prospect staff, their roles and motivations;
- gaining commitment to a survey of the prospect's operation;
- identifying needs and priorities;
- developing a solution;
- cost justifying the solution;
- obtaining agreement;
- submitting formal proposal;
- closing.

Major prospects

- Is there a pattern or sequence of activities leading to a major sale which is common to most prospecting situations? For example, identification of opportunities, pre-contact analysis, initial meetings, survey work, development of a solution, submission of formal proposal, follow up, decision.

- If there are variations to this pattern, what are they, and how often do they occur?

- Is there a formal system for planning and controlling progress from start to finish?

- If yes, is it used by the sales team (i.e. salespeople use it to help them sell and sales managers use it to help them direct and control sales activity)?

- Does this system cover both quantitative aspects of the process (e.g. number of prospect calls, conversion rate of proposals to orders) and the qualitative aspects (e.g. are the right people being contacted, what are their needs and priorities)?

- If a system exists but has fallen into disuse or partial use, have any steps been taken to ascertain why (e.g. wrong system, bad management, too flexible)?

- Have all the staff involved in using the system been trained and motivated sufficiently to use it?

- Does the design of the system make it a sales aid?

- If no system exists or if it has fallen into disuse, has any view been taken on the 'pros and cons' of having a system?

- Have the value and costs of major sales been calculated? For example, major sale value, major sale costs, number of calls, cost per call, total cost per sale, number of major opportunities pursued in a year, total major sales costs, sales management costs, sales support costs, total sales costs, total major sales revenue, total sales/sales per cent.

- Does the development of a major sale involve several levels of management and different departments?

- Putting the two points immediately preceding the previous one together, how important is it to have and use a formal control system for major sales?

- What planning precedes initial contacts on high-level decision-makers?

- How many different kinds of objective could be set for initial contacts? (NB: Ten possibilities would not be uncommon, although clearly not all ten would be set for one visit.)

- If you are managing major sales activity carried out by others, how do you know what objectives are set?

- Are the objectives specific, measurable, commercially worth while and capable of achievement?

- Are the objectives set with the right contacts?

- Are key customer contacts identified by their importance to the sale (i.e. decision-maker, recommender, influencer)?

- Is it known whether these contacts will accept or reject proposals for financial, functional or performance reasons?

- Are the attitudes and motivations of the contacts known?

- Are they contacted? It is often the case that many different departments are involved in a buying decision, but the sales-people only see the buyer and their immediate colleagues and, as a result, receive a skewed picture of their overall priorities.

- Is the sales team aware of all the internal resources available to it (i.e. people, equipment, services, materials)?

- When conducting a major sale do sales staff identify which internal resources they will need?

- What is the current state of the relationship between field sales staff handling major sales situations and internal support staff?

- Do the salespeople responsible for major sales recognise the value of involving internal resources?

- Do the internal support staff recognise the importance of major prospects?

- In addition to having the necessary business knowledge and investigating skills to create a major sale, are sales staff aware of the difference between tangible and intangible benefits?

- Can they spot opportunities to help the prospect obtain the tangible benefits of increased revenue or cost avoidance?

- Can they identify possible intangible benefits which, in the final analysis, may prove to be the most persuasive?

- Before preparing a solution, does the sales team get confirmation from the prospect that his needs and priorities really are as identified during the survey stage?

- Are we satisfied with the present conversion rate of prospects: orders in the major sales category?

- If not, where do the problems lie – in understanding the process, managing and controlling it, using it, or in sales staff's planning?

Existing major customers

- How is business with existing major customers planned?

- Is major customer planning an integral part of the company's annual planning process?

- Is information available on an individual customer basis to prepare individual plans?

- Do the formats cover both quantitative and qualitative information and actions?

- What formats are used for planning?

- Is individual customer profitability information available?

- Is it possible to compare individual major customers using a common format, and also to compare one customer segment with another?

- Are sales, cost and profit objectives set for major customers?

- Are broad strategy statements drawn up which will ensure customer satisfaction and competitive superiority?

- Are these strategies translated into specific action plans covering contacts to be made, call objectives, timing and support requirements?

- Is full use made of all internal resources?

- Is progress monitored?

- Have major accounts salespeople been trained in preparing customer strategies?

- Is the plan and strategy used to direct staff activities?

Cost-justifying solutions to customers' needs

A company making industrial components submits a quotation to a potential customer for 500 units at £100 each, on which the manufacturer makes a gross profit of 40 per cent, or £20,000. But the buyer indicates that he is only prepared to pay £90 per unit, although he can place a larger order. If the salesperson has been instructed to make a minimum gross profit of £20,000 on the deal, he has to respond by selling 667 units, dropping his profit to 30 per cent.

Is it right, though, to make the £20,000 the prime objective? There are other strategies. One would be to have an annual net profitability target for this customer, and view volume and price as just two of the ingredients of the negotiable relationship, the rest including delivery method, amount of technical support, invoice currency and payment period. In such a case, the gross profit could be amended up or down according to concessions given or obtained in other areas.

Another possibility, which could be used at the outset, would be to try to justify the original price. The following checklist examines cost-justifying solutions to customers' needs; an element in the conduct of major sales that is now critical to all companies, whether selling or buying.

In the recent UK recession, stagnant or declining demand has created a wealth of unused capacity, forcing up unit costs which cannot be recouped by higher prices because of the need for volume. With stocks moving slowly and customers taking extended credit, companies are working to the limit of their overdraft and paying heavy interest charges. The squeeze on margins means that for industrial companies, whose main tactical means of communication is their sales force, financial selling ability is not so much an extra string to the salesperson's bow as a lifeline for all other employees.

In considering how to beat the competition, salespeople know that buyers have less business to offer and more power to extract concessions. In their own company, too, they have to contend with production managers seeking to reduce unit costs without impairing product quality, R&D managers trying to keep development programmes running on fiercely reduced budgets, personnel managers wanting to maintain or improve performance skills on a training budget that is only a fraction of what they recommended, finance managers grasping every opportunity to minimise bank overdrafts and marketing men unwilling to spend money on any promotion which cannot be seen to have a direct effect on sales.

But finance is still something of a closed book to many people doing a selling job. For example, the very personality attributes that characterise the career salesperson are often not collusive to a facility with figures, just as many bank managers complain that they didn't go into banking in order to sell. People with a high degree of empathy are often attracted to selling jobs and by the same token find analytical work not just irksome but difficult. Paradoxically, however, it is mastery of figures which enables the person with natural social skills to use their talents to the full.

The need for financial selling has also been increased by continuing developments in distributive systems, technology and computerisation. Whereas packaging buyers, say, used to want information on product specification, prices, delivery and so on, they now seek help on the use of packaging design as a marketing tool. Salespeople, then, need multiple contacts with their customers and prospects, not simply with the buying department.

But three factors often limit effectiveness. To begin with, the sales role may be restricted to selling in to the buyer, thus preventing salespeople identifying other functional needs they may be able to satisfy. In addition, any lack of financial skill and general business awareness may lead to an inability to multiply the effects of an apparently minor product advantage – for example, how a slight difference in product specification will not only reduce reject rates, but reduce raw material stock requirements, cut bank overdraft and interest charges, increase machine output, lower costs per unit and create greater customer satisfaction, leading to higher volume and justifiably higher prices. Finally, we may lack a system for analysing customer situations comprehensively and financially.

Overall, there are key steps to making major customer approaches work. The first is to recognise that where major sales are concerned, customers want suppliers who can offer them bottom-line solutions. This means ensuring that salespeople have the breadth and depth of customer and prospect knowledge to identify profitable opportunities and to demonstrate supplier superiority; account planning skills to ensure that customer relationships proceed purposefully for both parties; and a control system which is an aid to the salespeople and a progress chart for the manager.

The second step is for salespeople to become well equipped with financial selling skills so that they match their wares to the financial requirements of a wide spectrum of functions within each customer's operations.

By adopting this approach, we increase our chances of being viewed genuinely as business partners by the prospect's key decision-makers, which is essential not only for the first sale but for subsequent success.

The next checklist sets out the factors affecting cost justification.

Major prospects

- How many departments within a major prospect's organisation can be affected by a decision to purchase the kind of products/services we supply?

- Who, within those departments, would be classified as decision-makers, recommenders or influencers?

- Do we, as a matter of course, contact these departments and the decision-makers, recommenders and influencers during the survey stage of the selling process?

- Does a system exist for conducting survey work to ensure all interested parties are contacted?

- Is the system formalised and documented or simply a suggested system for sales staff to follow?

- How well do our sales staff and others involved in major sales activities (like applications engineers) understand how the customer's departments operate?

- Do we know enough to be able to identify those customer activities that can be improved from purchasing our product?

- Can we translate these activities into specific improvement opportunities (like reduction in vehicle usage)?

- Can we relate these opportunities for improvements to specific aspects of our products/services?

- Can we identify the specific as opposed to the general benefits that result from purchasing our product/services?

- Can we describe these benefits (time/mileage/personnel numbers/material qualities, etc.) in figures, and do we do it?

- Can we put a financial value on the identified benefits (for example, given a reduction in mileage of 20,000 and an operating cost per mile of 30p, you will save £6,000)?

- Can we do these calculations for all the departments affected by the purchase of our type of product/service? For instance, would a cost reduction in production present an opportunity for sales volume increase at lower prices or an increase in margin at existing volumes?

- How do we know that it is done – do we have a formal system for ensuring that it is automatic on all major sales prospects?

- In making these calculations, do we dig for hard data from the prospect and sell him on the value of providing them?

- Where hard data does not exist, do we ask for and document specific estimates from the prospect?

- Where estimates are provided, do we recognise them for what they are and treat them with caution?

- Do our salespeople know the basic interviewing techniques to obtain estimates from prospects?

- Is there any evidence of our having lost sales through the promise of benefits we could not deliver?

- Having obtained all the necessary data, do we prepare a summary showing all the tangible benefits minus the costs of using our solution, and the resultant net position?

- What use do we make of intangible benefits, the ones that cannot be quantified?

- If we use them, do we ensure that they are benefits the prospect actually wants?

- Do we check that people in the prospect's organisation agree our calculations and will therefore give their support when the formal proposal is submitted?

- When did we last conduct a detailed training-needs analysis of staff involved in creating major sales?

- Have circumstances changed since then to the extent that a fresh examination is required?

- To what extent was the training-needs analysis based on what customers and prospects want from salespeople, as well as on what we want?

- Was the training-needs analysis comprehensive and accurate? (A computer mainframe manufacturer identified the need to train its salespeople in financial techniques but overlooked their innate fear of accountants. After training in standard financial techniques the salespeople were still reluctant to contact customers' finance directors and had to undergo further training to overcome their fear by role-playing with finance directors of client and prospect companies.)

- In which financial techniques should our major sales team be competent so that it can cost-justify our proposals?

- When did we last check how many customers and prospects compared our sales performance with the competition?

- How often do we give prospects financial reasons to buy, whether in written form or face-to-face?

Putting it in writing

The process described so far is sequential and cumulative. We have to move from stage to stage, and the case presented builds, or should do, as the process continues. One stage that needs to be considered is the selling situation which demands a formal written proposal/quotation from suppliers before a decision is made. Good proposals are an integral part of the process in that they reflect what has been identified in the previous stages, confirming in the prospect's mind that at least one supplier can offer a unique and valuable solution.

This means that the content of the proposal should not come as a surprise, nor should it be a substitute for face-to-face persuasion, though it must sell. Its role is essentially that of a written confirmation, reinforcing conclusions that have already been mutually agreed between the salesperson and all his key contacts in the prospect's organisation.

Like other forms of persuasive communication, a good proposal will meet three criteria: its *sequence* will match the reader's sequence of decision-making; its *content* will be attractive to the readers and satisfy their needs; its *presentation* will enhance the content.

Whatever the format of the proposal, it must not be a weak link. It must be thought about and put together in the right kind of way. Proposals and presentations (another potential weak link) were reviewed in detail in Chapter 6.

Expanding major accounts

Just because it is big, it does not follow that it will remain big – as of right – still less that it will get bigger. Yet, expanding major accounts may be the most important area of growth for many companies.

This chapter's final checklist is therefore concerned with building the business relationship, and it also summarises the key points in managing the process by which major sales are created.

A continuous business relationship is simply a means to an end, namely customer and supplier satisfaction. For the supplier it means establishing and maintaining account control so that profitable sales from the account can be expanded in a less competitive environment. For the salesperson in particular, it also means regularly reviewing their activity within the account, and re-directing their efforts to other more profitable opportunities if they find that the time they are investing in the customer is no longer furthering their company's objectives.

If they are doing their job, the salespeople will have their fingers on their customers' business pulses all the time, maintaining the momentum of the initial sale, ensuring that pre-sale promises are post-sale realities, reporting on progress before being asked, monitoring competitive activities and identifying future priorities.

Thus you should, ultimately, reach the point where you have a defined role within the customer's long-range planning process. Some salespeople have gone even further and have had their names put on the customer's internal mailing list. Among the industries where this technique can be put to vital use are computers, office equipment – particularly at the more sophisticated end, materials handling, construction equipment – and information technology.

Running through the checklists in this chapter has been the theme of creating major sales, particularly those involving industrial goods and contract services, where the process leading to the sale typically contains the stages discussed. The problem facing more experienced sales people in obtaining, keeping and expanding major accounts, as expressed by senior sales and marketing managers, is not one of product knowledge or face-to-face skill, rather it is the absence of a systematic approach to the process and the lack of a format for making sure it is used. As a result, opportunities can be overlooked, key customer personnel are ignored, customer priorities are misinterpreted and solutions are sold on the wrong arguments.

Exhortation is not enough. Somehow an environment has to be created which enables sales teams to make the best possible use of their innate skills and, for most companies, that means translating the accepted sales process in their industry into a formalised structure and insisting on its use.

Existing major customers

- Is it both policy and practice to expand contacts at all levels within the customer's organisation?

- Do we continue to keep the customer's buying staff informed of our activities even when they do not have a direct involvement in some of them?

- What steps do we take to ensure that our own technical staff, sales office personnel and anyone else with direct customer contact understand our account strategy, know the part they play and are comfortable in it?

- Are these members of the team trained in spotting potential problems or opportunities?

- Is there any method of reporting to ensure that any such problems or opportunities are brought to the salesperson's attention?

- To what extent are competitive activities monitored? What competitive product/services are being used? How does the customer rate the competition in product/service performance, prices and terms, and all non-product price matters?

- Do we continue to educate ourselves in the customer's industry in general?

- Do we obtain the customer's regular publications such as the annual report, house journal and sales literature?

- Do we attend any of the customer's functions, such as the AGM or sales meetings?

- Do we sell him the benefits of our attending internal meetings on problems/opportunities where our products/services might help?

- Do we keep the customer informed of developments within our own organisation highlighting progress in any area that can affect business?

- Do we invite the customer to any of our functions?

- Do we try to get involved in the customer's long-range planning process?

- Do we have a system for monitoring the management of our major accounts regularly?

- If the key person responsible for the account moves on, do we ensure that his replacement has all the information and documentation to carry on where he left off?

- Do we as a matter of course send a thank-you letter to the decision-maker which is also a reminder of what must happen next?

- Do we carry out follow-up visits to ensure effective implementation?

- Do we continue to remind the customer of the benefits of purchase?

- Do we monitor and report on the results of our installed products/services automatically?

- Do we take the initiative in conducting informal and formal account reviews with the decision-maker and recommenders?

- If our product is sold by our direct customer to end-users, do we carry out any checks with them so that we can pre-handle any possible complaints?

- Do we arrange to meet any new customer staff who could influence future sales?

- If yes, do we brief them on the reasons for implementing our solutions, the benefits so far obtained and future plans?

If there is a reflex operating which ensures that major accounts get the treatment they deserve, then more sales will result as more satisfactory relationships build up. So the final checklist is for the company, to help make sure that the whole area of major sales is actioned systematically, in a way that will secure, protect and develop the business on a continuing basis.

Not all customers are big, and the total of the 'others' is not unimportant. Sales have to be achieved from both, and the customer mix has to be managed effectively, so that this definitely occurs.

The checklists in this chapter were originally drawn up by Peter Kirkby for a book I edited, titled *The Salesmanagement Handbook*, and thanks are due to the publisher, Gower Publications, for permission to adapt and reproduce the material here.

9

Making it Work

> The ability to simplify means to eliminate the
> unnecessary so that the necessary may speak.
>
> *Hans Hofmann*

In this chapter you will find a word of advice and my observations about implementation. If any book about the sales process, or any other skill for that matter, is to be useful – assuming you have read your way through to the summary rather than starting with it – then it must be put not only to good, but also to practical, use. The question is how?

Consider a different situation. You are, let us suppose, keen on some sport. Tennis or golf, perhaps. In a fit of financial recklessness, and a good commission payment this month, maybe, you book some lessons with the coach or professional at the local club, in the hope of improving your game. A poor tennis coach will usually start by getting you to play for a few minutes and observing what you do. Then they will pause and tell you *all* the things you are doing wrong. They mention your grip on the racket, your stance, etc. 'Now, have another go' they conclude, brightly. So, attempting to concentrate simultaneously on all the specific points made, you have another go. What happens? You are lucky if you can get the ball over the net at all. Your game gets worse. Concentrating on so much at the same time just does not work.

The good coach on the other hand, will mention one thing specifically. 'Maybe there are a number of things we can work on – let's look at the grip first and see if we can improve that.' You do; and it does. The same principles of improvement work elsewhere, and they work with selling.

Do not go to your next call and try to think consciously about everything you have read. There are too many variables. Review one or two things. Better still, make a list of those areas where you think there is 'fine-tuning' to be done, and review them progressively over a number of calls. You are the best coach you have got, certainly the only one who is always there. By all means take advice, information and experience from anyone and anywhere, and at least think about it. What you deploy, and how, is your decision.

Develop the habit of review, and fine-tuning will become a habit; you will constantly – regularly – be making small changes, improvements, to the detail of what you do. Then sales success – or at least an above-average success rate – can become a habit too.

The summary of key elements that create a 'sales edge' set out below, may help you remember what needs to be reviewed, and put together a list of your own priorities for review.

1. **Planning** You must be organised, see the right people, the right number of people, on the right frequency and manage the sales process.

2. **Preparation** There must simply be no such thing as an unplanned contact, and whether preparation takes 2 minutes or 2 hours, it must always happen.

3. **Understand the structure** You will do better at every stage if you have a clear idea of what should be going on overall.

4. **Manner** Salespeople are not universally welcomed; the right manner will help put you in the ranks of the professionals.

5. **Direction** Get hold of the meeting; run the kind of meeting *you* want and *they* find they like.

6. **Identifying needs** Find out more clearly, thoroughly and precisely what prospects want and why, and everything thereafter will be less difficult.

153

7. **Listening** This is vital for identifying needs, obtaining information and part of the image that needs projecting.

8. **Clarity** Nobody buys what they feel they are inadequately informed about; everybody appreciates clear guidance on something they anticipate being complex.

9. **Talk benefits** It focuses what is done on the customer and makes it more descriptive in their terms.

10. **Handling objections** Do it confidently and realistically and you build your image as a professional.

11. **Closing** If you cannot close you will never sell effectively.

12. **Write persuasively** Be as persuasive on paper as face-to-face; do not let this be a weak link.

13. **Formal presentation** Sell as effectively 'on your feet' to a group as across the desk; more and more customer situations demand it.

14. **Persistence** Maintain contact, chase for a conclusion, do not allow paranoia to affect you.

Afterword – *action for the future*

An optimist is someone who thinks
the future is uncertain.
Anon

For the future, selling is likely to become increasingly complex. If nothing else, the increasing sophistication of buyers will see to this. Selling has always attracted 'magic formula' solutions, often evidenced by a spate of new approaches and training methods concerned with improving sales effectiveness and commercial success. Psychologists, sociologists and behavioural scientists have all discovered 'new' and definitive systems. Instructional designers, film writers and packaged training specialists have all produced the 'best' approach to training. And, some opportunists (only a few fortunately) have used mass-promotional techniques, gimmicks that will transform an average salesman after a 2-hour session and a couple of simple phrases into a productive and profitable employee.

Whatever the methods proposed, the fundamental principles of selling – identifying needs, selling through benefits, proving the claims made – have not changed. These are still the reasons why sales are made and, when they are neglected, salespeople fail.

Selling has never been just a simple question of knowledge, but of skills and, what is more, of complex social skills. The best training will recognise this, developing sales skills so that desired changes in behaviour will take place. And that sales training cannot be effective unless it is directly related to the job to be done and realistically based. Too many approaches have been concerned with behavioural changes and techniques, so that the commercial purpose is all but forgotten.

Selling must always relate to the job in hand. Techniques need to be deployed in an individual way, meeting by meeting, customer by customer. Its success is dependent, perhaps above all, on a constant, conscious fine-tuning of technique which seeks to keep the salesperson up to date with economic, market and competitive changes. Such a review can incorporate anything which may add to the body of technique, provided any new element – behavioural psychology, transactional analysis or whatever – fits logically with the basic range of techniques. And logically from the customer's viewpoint too.

So, is it possible to summarise? The whole premis of this book has been that it is the totality of the process, and the detailed deployment of techniques, that is what makes for success; and particularly it is the details – and their precise execution – which can create an 'edge'. However, in conclusion, and without downgrading the importance of anything else, the following factors seem keys for the future at this time.

The Commercial Environment

This is what dictates the essential nature of selling and other marketing communication in a competitive economy: current economic trends; how and why pressures have occurred; what future changes can be expected; and how the selling role must modify itself.

It also assesses the psychology of interpersonal communication and examines how human behaviour is modified in the sales process. Selling has no relevance other than as a part of the commercial environment and must adapt to the changing nature of this over time.

The Marketing Direction

Selling is but one part of the marketing and promotional mix. It must reflect the company's aims and image. If marketing puts the company in the position of say, a technical leader, salespeople must project, clearly, this technical excellence. If the image is of caring, good service, a slipshod salesperson will destroy the effect in a moment. Marketing defines the company's or division's financial and marketing objectives, outlines the prime emphasis of marketing objectives, outlines the prime emphasis of marketing strategy and therefore clarifies the priority for activities within the selling function.

In other words, whatever sales people do must be done in the context of the company's marketing activity of which it is a part. As marketing activity changes, so sales approaches must adapt to remain an integral part of the mix.

The Buying Attitude

This is crucial since success in selling will be judged finally by the actions of the buyer, not the salesperson. So a detailed element of the sales approach begins with an analysis of the role and attitude of the buyer. An examination of the different types of function in which buyers may be working – purchasing, finance, marketing, distribution and so on – and the different types of purchase which can be made by these functions is important. It should identify how the priorities of importance change in different industries and different functions, and will identify simple systems of analysis if a multi-functional decision-making process makes this necessary.

Further review must show how buyers are judged by their companies, how these criteria have developed and are modified depending on the kind of purchase decision being made. The purpose of this is to ensure that the salesperson focuses firmly upon the true buying motivation, and plans his approach and tests assumptions early on.

Everything, but everything, in selling must have a customer orientation.

The Communication Skills

Selling is only a form of communication, albeit persuasive communication. It goes beyond simple face-to-face verbal communication. The particular uses of the telephone, the differences between group and individual communication, the effective use of visualisation and the structure and presentation of formal written communication in surveys, proposals and reports, all need to be considered and used to full effect.

Some things are both fundamental and key; and can certainly be a potential source of weakness. Here are some important examples.

Research and preparation

Here we need to ask what systems and records formats are most useful in achieving effective time-saving preparation for a call? What sources of information are of the greatest use? For example, research regularly shows that buyers consider many of the salespeople calling on them know little, or nothing, about the buyer's company, industry or processes.

Opening/questioning techniques

Which type and sequence of question leads to success? How do salespeople create barriers for themselves during the opening of an interview? How are the crucial factors of credibility and professionalism built or destroyed by salespeople at this time? Relevant behavioural techniques can be useful in these areas.

Benefit selling

This is always key, providing customer focus and increasing the genuine description that is contained in any explanation. The need is not simply to 'talk benefits', however, but to relate, translate and apply benefits to the particular industry, company and individual with whom you are faced in an interview. Unless this key creative activity is practised, then the presentation will always lack persuasive force. As has been said, the concept of benefits and features appears deceptively simple. It is easy to deploy it inadequately and, by not getting the best from it, dilute sales impact.

Providing proof

People are often suspicious of someone with something to sell. It is not enough to say something is the 'best thing since sliced bread', the reaction may simply be one of 'they would say that wouldn't they'. Successful selling demands proof.

In any company with hundreds or thousands of examples every year of successful sales transactions, you would expect that each salesperson would have a vast array of specific practical examples to prove his case whether in cost saving, time saving, quality of work, increase in management efficiency or whatever he is intending to sell. Surprisingly, this is not always the case. The salesperson must discover and show how evidence can be provided and how it can be documented and communicated.

Handling objections

Success here is dependent on rebalancing the argument. Although initial training may well have examined answers to objections based on price, fear, habit and so on, focus is seldom made on emotional aspects. These are crucial also, for even if the 'right' answers are given, if the handling in human relations terms is awkward then the solution fails to satisfy. The result is loss of confidence and lowering of motivation to buy. Consideration (and practice) must therefore be given to 'handling' as well as 'answering'.

Closing

Some pundits cast doubts on the need to close. It may not cause people to buy, but it is certainly important in converting interest into action. Closing works; only bad or hasty closing fails. Still, many salespeople still find a major psychological block in closing, they know selling is a matter of strike rate (no one wins them all), yet fear of personal rejection and social discomfort put them off. A conscious effort to take all this in your stride and use closing techniques appropriately will always improve strike rate, at least to some extent.

All the above are fundamental. Other factors have become more important in recent years, some seem likely to remain so and increase in importance. Others will no doubt be added. These 'additional' skills include the following.

Account analysis and approach planning

The whole process of defining the pre-contact analysis necessary to, for instance, identify top management objectives and priorities, using published and customers' sources of information and structuring a board-level discussion. Analysing a customer's operational and financial performance, then using your own company's resources, to cost-justify approaches; are all important.

Major account control

Large customers are not only bigger than others, they are different from others. They demand ongoing profit analysis, quantitative and qualitative definition of the company's position versus competition, constructing and running customer strategies and building operational and financial proof of the success of solutions, maintaining senior management contact with various levels of management – whatever will maximise sales from the most important of customers. For many, there is increasing polarisation between large and smaller customers and all this will only become more important over time.

Written persuasiveness

If you measure salespeople's effectiveness on a scale of, say, 1–10, whatever their score on face-to-face communication they will often be several points lower once they put things down in writing. Yet, as more weight is given in many major decisions to formal proposals, so salespeople must be more heavily involved in the writing process. The points covered in discussion and the justifications identified should constitute the main argument of the proposal. Thus you must know how to structure your words for ease of reading and for conviction. This area will only get more important as a way of differentiating competitors.

Presentation

The incidence of formal presentation is also an increasing trend. It is no longer enough to be persuasive 'across the desk'. Today's salesperson is likely to need to be as highly competent in the verbal and visual presentation of proposals to major potential customers 'on his feet'. He must be as skilful in dealing with groups as individuals. Often it is the quality of group presentation which will provide sales success in competitive situations of roughly equal services or products.

There are of course other skills such as negotiation, financial justification and selling through dealers, all of which may have increased relevance as different sectors of the market develop. Their relevance, and relationship with the more fundamental process, can only be judged from the market demand and need, and must be regularly examined against the current market and in the context of future changes.

None of these factors, all having an impact on sales effectiveness, can be overlooked. Nor should anyone in selling overlook factors affecting productivity, many of which can have a major impact on success.

Such self-management tasks as the following all contribute:

- giving priority to and focusing on the key activities, and setting priorities in terms of market segment, customers and product offerings;

- establishing the true potential of customers and prospect;
- ensuring personal sales work-load can meet the priorities;
- controlling time usage and reducing non-productive activities, planning and organising travel and territory;
- identifying opportunities to sell the range through existing customers;
- measuring achievement against profit/contribution results.

And again market conditions change the way in which all this works and has to be viewed constantly. Too often neither companies nor individuals review with care the definition of what the sales job really is in precise activity terms. It is not enough to say only that the job is 'to sell'.

Recognising that selling is a dynamic process, resolving to review and change as necessary every approach, every nuance if necessary, is the first step to success, and particularly to maintaining success. This attitude, and fine-tuning in a practical way, allows the salesperson to take advantage of change, and may well give the additional 'edge' of being ahead of the game.

If anything approaching a 'magic formula' exists to help make selling more effective, then it is this attitude of review, 'fine-tuning' and improvement. It does not just happen. It takes conscious effort. As the old saying has it, 'The trouble with opportunities is that they so often come disguised – as hard work.'

It is perhaps not realistic to expect it to be easy, but it is reassuring to find that it works. That is what makes it worthwhile (and gives us our final 'sales edge').

SALES EDGE 15 | Adaptability

- think about what you do
- regard it as dynamic and changing
- never believe there is one 'right' way
- fine-tune constantly
- deploy techniques as appropriate for individual customers
- have the confidence to succeed

One final, and overall, factor must be mentioned. Selling is a dynamic process. There is no 'right' way. What works today may not be right tomorrow. What works with one customer may not be right with another.

The best salespeople are those who accept this and work at it; those who understand the skills and techniques, and learn from experience and deploy their approach in a considered way throughout every contact so that it is right for the occasion.

Develop the habit of this kind of consciousness of action, and make 'fine-tuning' an integral part of your approach and you will increase your chances of getting more and better orders, and of getting them more often.

Make everything you do differentiate you as a professional

Index